Betsy
Brown
George ♡

Clown
for Circus & Stage

Mark Stolzenberg

Photographs by Neil Sapienza

Sterling Publishing Co., Inc.   New York
Oak Tree Press Co., Ltd. London & Sydney

BY THE SAME AUTHOR
Exploring Mime

Dedicated to Vivian Belmont, my performing partner, for her
hard work, discipline, professionalism and understanding

THE MODELS
Vivian Belmont
Brion Baton Black
Jennie Dembrow
Lou Dembrow
Marilyn Galfin
William Poag Hall
Virginia Heath
Ron Randon
Mark Stolzenberg
Valli West

Library of Congress Cataloging in Publication Data

Stolzenberg, Mark.
   Clown for circus and stage.

   Includes index.
   1.   Clowns. I. Title.
GV1828.S8   791.3'3   80-54337
ISBN 0-8069-7034-0   AACR2
ISBN 0-8069-7035-9 (lib. bdg.)

Contents

Acknowledgments

Special thanks to John Towsen and Fred Yockers of "If Every Fool . . ." Inc., and the "If Every Fool . . ." library collection, and to Fred Yockers for introducing me to the art of Clown.

I would like to thank Neil Sapienza, the photographer, for his patience, professionalism and support.

Thanks to Vince Monzo for the fun we had clowning together and for access to the Vince Monzo Stills Collection. Thanks to Mike and Beth Bongar and to Paul Binder.

Thanks to Jim Moore for his sincere efforts to preserve and re-vitalize the Variety Arts, and special thanks to the Board Members of the Hudson Street Studio, Inc. for their interest in my work and for their time and support.

Thanks to Francis and Claudine Belmont for their encourage-ment and help, and to Seymour and Arlene Stolzenberg, my parents.

I would like to acknowledge Jerry West for his insights into the Pueblo Indian Clowns. And thanks to Islene Pinder, Rebecca Rifkin, Peter Ronick, Rhona and Andy Goold, Leigh Scott, Lou and John Dembrow, Brion Black, Michael Muschen, Philippe Petit, Francis Bruun, Sharon Joyce, Jay and Helene Stolzenberg, Bernadette Fiorella, and Sheila Barry, my editor, and thanks to the people of New York City for supporting my street per-formances.

1
seriously clowning around

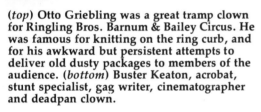

(*top*) Otto Griebling was a great tramp clown for Ringling Bros. Barnum & Bailey Circus. He was famous for knitting on the ring curb, and for his awkward but persistent attempts to deliver old dusty packages to members of the audience. (*bottom*) Buster Keaton, acrobat, stunt specialist, gag writer, cinematographer and deadpan clown.

(*top*) Oleg Popov—the famous Soviet clown—was a wire walker, juggler and pantomimist. He did a famous clown slack wire act where he supposedly fell asleep on the wire. (*bottom*) Lou Jacobs and his dog, Knucklehead. Master clown with Ringling Bros. Barnum & Bailey Circus, Lou Jacobs is a contortionist and plays several musical instruments. He is famous for his tiny car routine and his motorized bathtub (he built them both himself).

seriously clowning around

We each have a little clown inside us, waiting to pop out and express itself in a romantic and fun way. Using this book as your guide, you'll learn some of the basics of the art of Clown, as well as a process for discovering your own personal clown. This doesn't mean you simply put on makeup and a costume and jump around in an inspired "clown frenzy." Clown is a serious art form, and you need to approach it in a disciplined and systematic manner.

The art of Clown is often misunderstood.

Many people think clowns are meant to blow up balloons "for the children" at birthday parties, give out leaflets at shopping malls, or perhaps sell hamburgers on television. In fact, Clown is a traditional and complex art. It requires a great deal of practice and discipline to become a good professional clown. If you work hard, rehearse, and follow the suggestions in this book, you'll find fun and fulfillment as a beginner clown "seriously clowning around."

As a clown you can perform at festivals, parades and parties, in variety shows and stage productions. If you want to go on and perform professionally, there are opportunities in the theatre, in films, in commercials, and there are many small circuses and carnivals, where you can learn by performing.

Take a look at the pictures on page 9. Character #3 is obviously a clown because he's wearing the recognizable makeup and costume. However, the other 3 may be clowns, too, depending on what they do and how they do it.

1

2

3

4

Studying Clown will help you to be more expressive, open and communicative.

Mimes, musicians, singers, dancers and actors can all expand their range and benefit from the vulnerability and comic understanding of the clown. When a clown makes us laugh, he or she touches something deep inside our consciousness. Any artist will want to know how to do that.

It's difficult to define what a clown is, but you're sure to know a clown when you see one. A clown is an actor who uses movement, cartoon-like imagery, a distinct makeup and costume,

As a clown—

**you can play a
musical instrument—**   **ride a unicycle—**   **sing—**

10

rhythm—sometimes words—sound, satire, a variety of skills, and most important, a specific character to make people laugh. Clowns make stupid mistakes: they trip and fall down; they don't see obvious solutions to simple problems; they fight among themselves for silly reasons; and they make fools of themselves. People laugh at these things because they're performed in the style of comedy, and because it's easy to identify with the clowns. We all experience embarrassing and awkward situations in which we feel foolish, and everyone makes stupid mistakes from time to time.

and dance—   juggle—   recite Shakespeare—

The key is to use and integrate any skill you have to present and to serve your clown character. Character is the essential element of your clown, and your task is to discover the character that works best for you—a character you're comfortable with—and one which is funny and believable.

You'll learn how to develop and present your clown character as you follow the exercises in this book. As you explore different characters and techniques, make note of movements, ideas, feelings, character elements and anything else which seems to work

do Mime—   perform acrobatics—

well for you. It's a good idea to keep a notebook of ideas. When you experiment, certain things may "click" or feel right. You can get the most out of these feelings and sensations by writing them down so you can refer to them later as you develop your clown. Keep a loose-leaf binder divided into categories. Always carry around some paper or a small book or pad. When you get an idea, jot it down and then, when you have time, enter it into the loose-leaf binder in the appropriate section.

Here are some sample categories with notes:

Category	Sample Note
1. Funny Movements	Swivel hips back and forth
2. Character Ideas	High-pitched squeaky voice
3. Routines	Trick bicycle keeps falling apart
4. Costume and Makeup	Shoes too big
	Pants too short
5. Blow-Offs or Surprise Endings	Pull off long shirt and pants fall down
6. Funny Images	Clown with big hatchet stuck in rear end
	Smoke squirting out of ears
7. Miscellaneous	Little cop arrests big, tall clown

Create your own categories and make notes in any manner you like. This is important: good ideas are easily forgotten unless you write them down. Most professional clowns and comedians work this way.

Note: The photographs in this book are here to help you visualize and understand the way a clown performs. They'll give you an idea of how you can use your body and present yourself on stage. They'll also give you a feeling for clown characters and how to stage routines. But don't try to copy or imitate them exactly. They're only meant to be a guide, an example, a starting-place, from which you'll go on to create your own character and material. Always try for new and original ideas. Find ways to express yourself which are unique to your personality and the character you're developing. You'll always be funnier if you remain true to yourself.

or some combination thereof.

2
discover your hat

discover your hat

Discovering your hat is a key step toward discovering your clown. The type of hat you choose—and the way you wear and use it—is closely connected to your clown character. At this point, it isn't important to find the exact hat or permanent hat for your clown, but it is crucial that you become aware of:

☆ the importance of your hat—
☆ the many ways you can use your hat—
☆ how your hat relates to your clown image and character—
☆ the different clown hats and clown images you can experiment with.

In this chapter you'll experiment with techniques that help you discover your "hat." These will include:

The Projection of Attitudes—You need to learn how to express yourself with your entire body. Clowns who know how to work with their physical movements are funnier than others, and much more interesting to watch. In addition, when you "physicalize" and exaggerate your emotions, intentions, reactions and activities on stage, the audience will understand more clearly what you're doing.

Clown Walks—These express the absurdity of the clown. When you see Groucho Marx bend over and pace back and forth as he smokes his cigar, you know you're watching a clown and not a normal everyday human being.

The First Explorations of a Character and a Clown Image—Your clown character is the most important aspect of your clown. Your character is your clown's personality; it dramatizes who he or she is; and it includes the image of your clown. Your image is your costume, makeup and overall appearance. Working with hats is a good way to explore different kinds of characters.

A clown is not a normal, everyday individual.

A clown and his hat are like a boy and his dog. They belong together and have a complex relationship. A clown's hat is not just a hat; it can be:

a best friend—

an enemy—

a roof over your head—

a toy—

A hat can be:

an obstacle—   a handkerchief—   a steering wheel—

a trusty weapon—   a pacifier—

17

A hat can be:

a symbol of wealth—

a symbol of poverty—

an old reliable acquaintance—

a pillow—

a sex object—

a costume—   and more.

Projection of Attitudes

An attitude is a frozen pose, statue or snapshot of a clown in the midst of action. The clown may be showing an emotion or an intention; he or she may be thinking or caught in the middle of doing something. Clowns often slow down or freeze in the midst of a routine and hold a pose. You need to work on developing your attitudes and projecting them so that:

☆ Audiences can see what you're doing—
☆ You learn to express yourself with your entire body—
☆ You become more aware of yourself as a performer—aware of the different types of attitudes you can show and how they look to an audience—
☆ You begin to discover the style and exaggeration needed to perform as a clown—
☆ You can experiment with and discover your hat—
☆ You develop a unique clown character that suits you.

Run around the room, shaking out your arms and legs. Try to be really loose as you run. Make plenty of noise, too, any sounds you feel like making.

Then suddenly freeze. All commotion stops. Don't move a muscle. You are frozen like a rock. Try not to let anyone see that you're breathing.

"Sophisticated" with too much tension

Now run around again, and again freeze. Freeze in any position you land in. You should be perfectly still on the outside, like a statue. But you mustn't be a dead statue. On the inside you're bubbling with life. Imagine that you're about to explode into action, like a tiger waiting to pounce on its prey. On the inside you are vibrant with energy; on the outside you're perfectly still.

It's important to keep the vibrations and energy going inside. This inner life is a key to projecting your attitudes. Whenever you perform, keep that energy going inside, like a twinkle. Try to touch your audience with it.

Specific Attitudes

Now try to become a statue which represents the word *sophisticated*. Take your time. Imagine that you're a statue in the park, a statue that people would recognize as "sophisticated" immediately, even though it had no title. Hold the statue and try to project this attitude to the other end of the universe. Make sure you're using your entire body. Project energy from every pore. This does *not* mean to tense up. You can project without too much muscular contraction.

Now, relax. Do the same thing for the word *obscene*. Exaggerate the attitude. Try to express the essence or spirit of the word, rather than its literal meaning.

Now switch from "sophisticated" to "obscene" in slow motion. To do this, move extremely slowly at one constant speed until you reach the "obscene" position. After you reach "obscene," hold this attitude for about 10 seconds. Then slowly switch back to "sophisticated."

Next, switch from "sophisticated" to "obscene" in one short, sharp, quick, staccato movement, and back to "sophisticated" in the same staccato rhythm.

Whenever you move from one attitude to another, you should know exactly where you're going. Try to visualize the lines in space through which you must move to reach your new position.

"Sophisticated" with too little tension

"Sophisticated" with the right amount of tension

And "Obscene"

Duets

1. Select a pair of attitudes. Stand next to your partner and each of you assume one of the attitudes.

2. In slow motion, you both switch attitudes. Wait a few seconds and switch back to your original positions, again in slow motion.

Now do the same thing to a staccato rhythm.

Next repeat that duet, but this time one of you will initiate or start the movement. The other partner responds by switching also, but it should look as though the initiator is causing the other person to change position.

3. Do the duet again. This time try to find a reason for switching positions. In the illustration, using the words "playful" and "pugnacious," the initiator decides to hit the partner. The partner reacts by giggling.

Try the same exercise with the following attitudes:
Proud—Humble Extroverted—Shy
Angry—Afraid   Happy—Unhappy
Serious—Joking

Clown Walks

Most clowns have an identifiable and stylized clown walk or way of moving. Your walk, of course, is closely connected to your attitudes, your overall image, and the nature of your clown character.

This doesn't mean that you must walk in a predetermined, stylized or clownish manner. It means that your walk will be a strong pattern in your movements, and you will use it often. People will associate your clown with your walk, the way they do with Charlie Chaplin and Groucho Marx.

22

Developing a Clown Walk

1. Pick an attitude from page 21 and hold it for 10–15 seconds. Find a way to walk around the room in that attitude, as if you're a statue come to life. Change your body position, if you want, so that you may walk more easily, but keep the spirit and essence of your attitude.

2. After a minute or two, think of an animal—any animal—and add one or two of its characteristics to your walk. If you think of an ape, for instance, you might let your arms hang loose and slouch a bit. It's more important to add the feeling and spirit of the animal than very specific attributes. For example, you might change the rhythm of your walk to that of the animal.

3. Now think of a person you know or one that you've seen. Add some quality, characteristic, or any other aspect of the person to your walk. Make sure you maintain the qualities you've already developed—the attitude and animal—as you work.

4. At this point you've created a rather peculiar creature walking around your room. Select a song which fits the creature's personality and sing it in the creature's voice as you continue. Let the rhythm of the song affect the way you're walking.

Your Hat

Continue walking as you were. Stop singing your song and just hum it to yourself. Let the song fill your walk with life and rhythm. Now pick a hat—any hat—put it on your head, and start thinking of your creation as a clown character.

Start again from page 21 and develop another walk. Use a different attitude, animal, person, song and hat.

This clown is working on a walk and a character using "obscene" as the attitude, the ape as the animal, Marlon Brando for the person, and "The Eensy-Weensy Spider" for the song.

More on Hats

Select 6–10 different hats. For each one:

1. Look at the hat carefully. Then very quickly place it on your head and, without thinking about it, immediately go into a clown walk. The key to this exercise is to be spontaneous. Just do whatever comes into your mind, or allow whatever impulses are felt by your body.

2. Stand in front of a mirror—a big, full-length mirror, if possible—and repeat that exercise. This time, observe yourself. See how each hat makes you look and feel.

3. Pick one of the hats and use it for at least 5 different purposes, to say hello, for example, or to kill a fly.

4. Select an attitude and assume it in front of a mirror. Try on different hats, but maintain the exact body position and attitude for each hat. See if a different hat makes any change in the meaning of your attitude.

Remember, a clown is a person—not an animal or creature—so eliminate any distorted or very weird-looking characteristics which don't seem to fit the spirit of a clown. You're trying to be a cartoon-like character (left), not (right) a tragic victim of some disease.

3
how to say hello

how to say hello

The beginning and the end of a clown routine are strategically important parts of a clown act. They are like a package or container which holds the routine together. When you enter, you present yourself to the audience for the first time. If you make a good impression, the audience will be attentive and receptive to what you do next. Clown is different from the other performing arts in that a clown always can break through the formality of the performer-audience relationship and acknowledge the audience directly.

After a clown enters, the next activity introduces the character: it says "Hello" to the audience. You might literally say the word "Hello," or you could do something else to say hello symbolically, like tipping your hat or smiling.

The end of a routine is important because it leaves a last impression with the audience. The audience will remember you from your exit.

As you work on these parts of your clown act, you'll also learn how to center yourself and something about stage presence and the vulnerability of the clown.

The Entrance and Exit

Making entrances and exits is very easy. To enter, walk, run, dance or move in any way you like from the off-stage area to the playing area, where you can be seen by the audience. To exit, leave the playing area and thereby end your part in the routine. Both the entrance and the exit should be strong, emphatic in their rhythm, and simple. Use a clown walk on your entrance and exit, if you want to, and if it fits logically into your routine. It's also a good idea to use your hat in some way from the start.

The exit can be similar to the entrance or very different. Often clowns exit in a chase or after a surprise ending, and the exit is determined by the logic and rhythm of the routine. You may have to carry props off-stage as you exit. This will affect the way you move, walk, or run. You may even have to pick up props from the floor to clear the stage for the next act. If another clown has just ripped your pants off, your exit will be very different than it would be if someone were chasing you with a giant foam rubber mallet.

As a clown, you'll be working either in a circus ring or on a stage. Use the diagrams on the next page for reference. They'll help you with the logistics of entering the playing area and staging your routines. Playing or performing in a circus ring is different from playing on a stage. When you block or choreograph your clown routine, you have to be conscious of whether it will be performed on a stage or in the circus ring. Most routines can be adapted easily from one to the other, but the ring is generally more difficult to work in, since the audience surrounds you. On a stage, the audience is usually in one downstage direction.

In an emergency, you might even have to carry another clown off-stage when you exit.

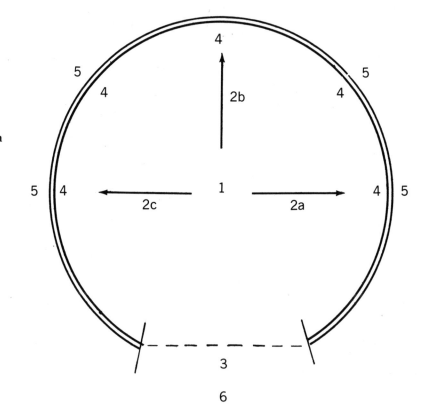

A. Circus Ring

1. Center Ring
2. a—Right Side of Ring
   b—Straight out
   c—Left Side of Ring
3. Entrance Area with Curtain
4. Ring Curb
5. Audience
6. Off-stage Dressing Area

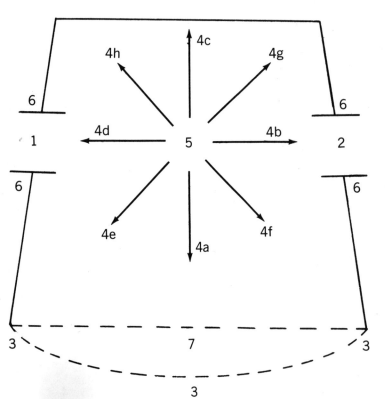

B. Proscenium Stage

1. Stage Right—Wings
2. Stage Left—Wings
3. Audience
4. a—Downstage—Downstage Center
   b—Stage Left
   c—Upstage—Center
   d—Stage Right
   e—Downstage—Right
   f—Downstage—Left
   g—Upstage—Left
   h—Upstage—Right
5. Center Stage
6. Torms (masking)
7. Apron

Staging Your Routine

Try to become aware of the lines you create on stage—or in the ring—when you move from one place to another. After you've experimented for a while—and know exactly where you want to move and when—you're ready to set the staging or blocking. Keep it simple and direct. Beginner clowns tend to move too much. When you express an idea, emotion or intention, do it as efficiently as possible (unless you're exaggerating a pattern for comic effect). Cut out unnecessary movements and make sure the ones you keep are clear and carefully timed.

How to Say Hello

Let's take a simple "hello." It's made up of an entrance, the "hello" itself, and an exit. First select a hat and a character, as you did in Chapter 2, and work on a simple entrance. The way you make your entrance depends, in part, on what you'll be doing after your entrance. For example, let's imagine you're sneaking on stage to perform a magic act. You aren't scheduled to perform, but you—that is, your clown character—really want to try out a new trick. Tiptoe on stage very quietly. Take big steps and exaggerate your fear of being discovered. (This is your entrance.) Now, slowly turn to the audience, put your index finger to your mouth and, in a large gesture, say "Shhhhhhh!" Bend your legs and become smaller as you say "Shhhhhhh!" (This is your "hello.")

Next, you think you hear somebody coming, so stop—listen carefully—become afraid, and then quickly run off-stage. (This is your exit.)

Hello Again

Here's another "hello." Run on stage very quickly. You are frantically looking for your partner. (This is your entrance.) Stop, look at your watch, realize it's late, look out to the audience in despair, and then show the audience how angry you are at your partner. (This is your "hello.") Finally, march off-stage in a huff. (Your exit.)

Look at the diagrams on page 34 for a simple way to stage your "hello" for the stage and for the circus ring.

One way of saying "Hello"

Stylizing Movements

When you perform your entrance, "hello" and exit, remember to exaggerate your movements and gestures.

Here are two ways to look at your watch and realize it's late:

Ordinary movement   **Stylized movement**

In the pictures on the right, the clown is exaggerating and using his entire body. This is called *stylizing* the movements. Whenever you perform as a clown, stylize your movements and gestures by making them big, simple, and easy to understand. Use your entire body to express yourself.

There are many ways to make an entrance, say "hello" and exit. The way you say "hello" depends on your character, what your character wants, what your character does to get it, and the nature of the routine you're performing. More about this in Chapter 6—"How to Get What You Want."

Here are some ways and reasons for entering:

☆ to escape from your partner
☆ to look for your pet dog
☆ to swat a fly
☆ to perform a dangerous feat
☆ to wander in, innocently

There are many ways to say "hello," too. Here are a few more:

☆ laugh
☆ play a note or short melody on an instrument
☆ shyly turn to the audience and smile
☆ tip your hat
☆ take a bow
☆ wave hello
☆ sing a short song
☆ sneeze

You can also exit in many ways:

☆ run off in fear
☆ run off to go to the bathroom
☆ look for your dog
☆ shyly excuse yourself

Explorations

Try these explorations on your own:

1. Make an entrance, say "hello," and exit 3 more ways.

2. Enter, say "hello," and exit twice. The second time, change the way you say "hello," but keep the same entrance and exit.

3. Enter and say "hello" 2 more times. The second time, change your entrance and exit, but keep the same "hello."

Centering and Vulnerability

The clown is an actor, a very broad actor. As a clown you need stage presence, but at the same time you must remain *open* to the audience. When you said "hello" to the audience in the previous exercise, you opened yourself to the audience. This means that you let the audience know what you were feeling or thinking by expressing yourself directly. When you are open, you interact with the audience. You might respond to something someone in the audience says or does. This openness adds to the vulnerable quality that clowns often have. The audience will sympathize with you if you're vulnerable. This means you must be receptive—and respond genuinely—to things which go on either in the audience or on the stage. If someone in the audience yells something out loud at you, you can respond with an angry look or an embarrassed smile or in many other ways. In general, a clown is a "bigger-than-life" performer. You must be convinced that you're charming and special. You must "seduce" the audience with your character.

The following exercise will help you develop a sense of center and improve your presence on stage. Only when you're centered and relaxed will you be able to let yourself be vulnerable and responsive to the audience. This, in turn, will allow you to interact with the audience and be spontaneous.

Centering Yourself

Stand in second position (as shown in illus. 1). Imagine that you're being pulled up from the top of the back of your head, so that your back is straight. Imagine a straight line from the top of your head to the base of your spine. Keep your legs straight; your shoulders back, down and relaxed; your chest out. Let your arms hang loosely at your sides. You're not afraid, nor are you pushing a phony bravado. Just be there.

Raise your arms and take a deep breath on a 6-count.

Lower your arms on a 6-count as you exhale.

1

2

A clown must have a strong center. This frees you to take risks and be a little outrageous. Do other exercises which you know relax you, clear your mind, and energize your system before you rehearse or perform. Try the warmup exercises at the end of the book.

Mime and dance classes will help to develop your presence, too, and of course there's no substitute for experience. The more you rehearse and perform, the more confident you'll be on stage. Concentration on stage will also help you relax and be less self-conscious. In the following chapters, you'll learn some acting techniques which require a great deal of concentration and focus. This focus and the use of your imagination when you act will reduce the awkward feeling you may have sometimes when you're on stage. Performing is a game to be played to its fullest and enjoyed.

As you inhale and exhale, imagine that you're sending out energy to the audience, and that this energy is growing deeper, wider and stronger. Feel it connect to things around you: the furniture, the walls, the ceiling. Touch the back of the room or rehearsal space with your vibration. Now feel the ground under your feet and concentrate on the sensation of gravity keeping you firmly planted on the floor. You are at home, that is, natural and relaxed.

3

4

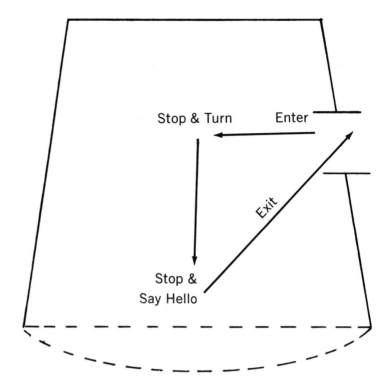

An example of an Entrance-Hello-Exit for the stage

Stop & Turn ← Enter

Stop & Say Hello

Exit

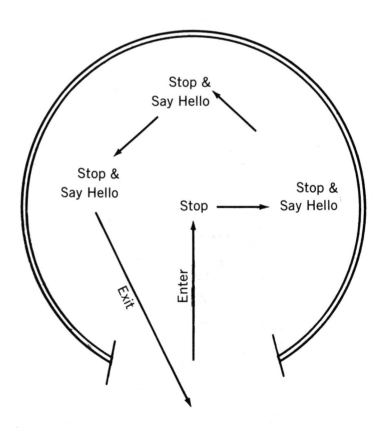

An example of the same staging for the ring

Stop & Say Hello

Stop & Say Hello

Stop → Stop & Say Hello

Exit

Enter

4

who is your clown?

who is your clown?

Traditionally, there are three major types of clowns:

☆ the Whiteface Clown
☆ the Auguste Clown
☆ the Character Clown

It's up to you to use these character types to create your very own personal and unique clown.

As you've seen, character is the most essential element of the clown. All your clown's actions and responses, thoughts and feelings—even your skills—are projected to the audience through your clown character. That character, plus a little bit of imagination and some funny skit ideas, will give you your clown.

Francois Fratellini, whiteface clown of The Fratellini Brothers, a highly respected French clown trio.

The Whiteface Clown

The whiteface clown is sophisticated, graceful, shrewd and aristocratic. He or she classically wears an elegant costume and, of course, a whiteface makeup. The image the whiteface projects is like a cartoon—something from another world —a fantasy.

George Footit (1864-1921), an authoritarian whiteface clown.

In modern terms, the whiteface can be called "the straight man." He is the one who appears to be serious and proper. The whiteface represents authority, and often the character is very severe. Generally, as you can see by his actions, the whiteface is very cultured, charming, and knows all the social graces. The French call the whiteface a "clown debonaire."

The whiteface usually works with a partner, the "auguste clown."

The auguste part of the Fratellini team, Albert Fratellini.

The Auguste Clown

"Auguste" in German means "stupid." The auguste clown is the "dumb-dumb." Over the years the image of the auguste evolved from the simple exaggerated character makeup and costume to a more grotesque, colorful, baggy-pants-ed and big-nosed clown.

37

The auguste is the clown who seems to do everything wrong. He trips over himself, interrupts and disturbs the whiteface (or the ringmaster), and often disrupts the activities of the whiteface. There is usually conflict between the whiteface and the auguste. For instance, suppose the whiteface enters and announces that he is going to give a concert on his violin. The auguste might enter just as the whiteface begins to play and attempt (noisily) to construct a big chair so that he can sit comfortably and enjoy the concert. This would be the beginning of a conflict in which the auguste would continually interrupt the concert.

In general, the auguste's simplicity, stupidity, charm and naiveté make him a sympathetic character, while the whiteface's pomposity gives you the feeling that he deserves to be interrupted.

The auguste's mannerisms are exaggerated, absurd, and unpredictable. He finds the most simple tasks—like putting his hat on his head—difficult. But on the other hand, the auguste is very skilled, and often finds complex acrobatic ways to solve simple problems. For example, he might walk on his hands and dip his head into his hat to get it on his head, instead of simply bending down to pick it up.

The whiteface-auguste relationship is used by many modern-day comics, comedians and clowns. Take Abbott and Costello, for instance. Abbott is the whiteface, Costello the auguste. With George Burns and Gracie Allen, George is the whiteface, Gracie is the auguste. The same with Mindy and Mork: Mindy is the whiteface, Mork the auguste. With Bugs Bunny and Elmer Fudd, Bugs is the whiteface, Elmer the auguste.

Doug Ashton, veteran tramp clown, is a master of comic timing, improvisation and slapstick. His costume and makeup are similar to Chaplin's.

The Character Clown

The character clown is an exaggerated or stock character, a caricature of people in everyday life.

Some examples of character clowns:

☆ a nurse with a big bosom and a big rear end—often
played by a man—
☆ a nutty professor—
☆ a tramp or hobo—
☆ a washerwoman or cleaning lady.

The tramp clown, like Charlie Chaplin or Emmett Kelly, became popular during the Depression when there were many tramps and bums travelling around the country. A modern-day version of the tramp clown is the shopping-bag lady clown which has recently become popular.

If you want to develop a character clown, study unusual people you see around you. Pick an interesting one and try to create a clown character from there.

John Towsen and Fred Yockers are a modern clown duet. Like Laurel & Hardy, their costumes and makeup look similar, and they relate to each other like a whiteface-auguste team.

(*top*) Valli West portrays a modern whiteface clown. The modern whiteface is not necessarily the authoritarian straight-man that the traditional whiteface is. Ms. West's character, like the cartoon character Olive Oyl, is young, feminine, shy and silly. (*bottom left*) Virginia Heath uses exaggeration in the size of her costume to help create a modern auguste clown. Her clown character is goofy and uses very large exaggerated movements. (*bottom right*) Vivian Belmont works as a character clown, a satire of a middle-class housewife. Her character is grumpy, overworked, cynical and fed up, but she retains a childlike, foolish quality. The contradiction of the adult, overburdened with responsibility, who harbors a foolish child inside, helps her to create comedy.

Clown Image

Many clowns are not pure whiteface, auguste or character clowns, but combine elements of the 3 traditions. For example, a clown might have a whiteface makeup but dress and behave like an auguste clown. Experiment with different images for your clown: the image consists of makeup and costume combined with character and movement qualities. Think of your clown as a cartoon come to life. The most important thing about your image is that it serves to project your character and helps to express the kinds of things your character does.

You'll work on your clown image in more detail in Chapter 16. Meanwhile, think about and experiment with costume and makeup ideas. That will help you discover who your clown is and develop its character.

Here are pictures of more clowns. Note their costume, makeup and overall image.

Clown Biographies

As you create a character, it's important to know *who the character is* and what his or her life is like. Many actors write pages of fictitious biographical information about the lives of the people they're playing. This helps create a clown character because it provides:

☆ a source of details and poetic images about the character which you will use when playing your clown—
☆ belief in the clown character—first for you, then for your audience—
☆ information which will help you make choices and decisions about what your clown's actions should be—
☆ an aid in figuring out how your clown fits into scenarios or skits—
☆ information from which you can create your *clown image*.

Invent a Life

Write a short biography—2–5 pages—for each of the 3 classical types of clowns: the whiteface, the auguste, and a character clown. Using these brief descriptions as a starting point, let your imagination take over. Have fun making up backgrounds for your clown. Put down anything that pops into your head. Feel free to exaggerate. Inventing these details will add to your belief in the character, and you'll use this information when you work on portraying your clown.

Include the following data in each biography:

- ☆ birthdate and astrological sign
- ☆ place of birth
- ☆ family life
- ☆ father's and mother's occupations
- ☆ important childhood experiences
- ☆ hobbies
- ☆ social class
- ☆ political and religious values
- ☆ favorite foods
- ☆ physical weaknesses and strengths
- ☆ vulnerable body parts

More on Character Background

Think of a clown character, like Charlie Chaplin's, Stan Laurel's, or Red Skelton's, and write a short biography that tells what you think the character's past was like.

No one will see your character notes but you, so write whatever you like. These are your private notes and you can let your imagination take over.

5
clown fantasies

clown fantasies

Your imagination plays a vital part in creating your clown. It allows you to visualize ideas and pictures; colors and textures; rhythms, objects and people; and to recall sensory experiences: sounds and tastes, odors and body sensations. You can tap all kinds of images in your mind which will help you create your clown. The following explorations will guide you through some imaging experiences. Later you'll apply these imagination skills to a specific clown character.

Here's Egg in Your Face

Imagine that someone has smashed a raw egg on top of your head.

> How does it feel?
> Is it warm or cold?
> Feel it drip down your neck and into your shirt.
> What particular part of your body is most uncomfortable?
> Do you smell anything?

Go look at yourself in an imaginary mirror. As you can see, you're a mess. Create an imaginary towel. Know its size and shape, its texture and color. Is it fresh? Does it have an odor? Now clean yourself up with it.

Look Out a Window

Create an imaginary window overlooking a street. Decide the size, shape, color, texture and other details about your window. Open it, look outside and *see* a street scene: people, cars, dogs, children. What's the weather like? What do you hear? Someone zooms by on roller skates. Something funny happens; you laugh. As you bring your head back inside, you accidentally bump it on the window. Where does it hurt?

45

Walk Through a Garden

Imagine a huge garden on an estate. What do you see?

How many flowers?
What kinds? What colors?
What do you smell?
What are the trees and shrubbery like?
Is there a walkway in the garden? What is it like?
Do you hear anything?
What season of the year is it? What's the weather like?
Try to figure out if it's going to rain.

Now walk through the garden *as if*:

☆ You're the Prince who owns it—
☆ You're a drunken servant—
☆ You're a mischievous 6-year-old boy—
☆ You're the old man who has been caring for the garden for the last 30 years.

As If

As if is a very important phrase. It sets you up to use your imagination. You'll do many things, as a clown, *as if* certain conditions—usually imaginary ones—are affecting you.

Immediate Circumstances

As a clown you must create the immediate circumstances and details surrounding a skit. Most clown scenarios are very general, and you have to fill in the details. So use your imagination and rely on the *as if* principle. You have the opportunity to be very creative, flexible, and to experiment with many possibilities. It's up to you to discover what works best for your clown.

The Referee

Imagine that you are the referee at a boxing match. Make an entrance, say "hello" (see Chapter 3), introduce the match and the boxers, and make an exit.

Before you begin, use your imagination to:

☆ discover a hat for the referee—
☆ discover a clown walk—

☆ write a biography of the referee—
☆ create the boxing ring, boxers, arena and spectators.

You can add to the humor of the situation by doing your actions *as if* specific *immediate circumstances* are affecting you. You might imagine one of the following:

**This is your first
referee assignment.**

**You are nearsighted,
and left your glasses home.**

**You have to go to
the bathroom badly.**

There is a beautiful
woman in the audience;
you are flirting.

You have just eaten
too much dinner.

Some combination of
these circumstances.

The Waiter

Use your imagination to pantomime a short scene in which
you're a waiter in a crowded restaurant. First, create for yourself
all the details of the restaurant.

Where are the tables?
Describe some of the customers.
How many tables are you waiting on?
Are they near each other?

Describe the details of the restaurant's ambience.

What is the lighting like?
What color is the floor?
Where is the kitchen?
What's on the menu?

On this particular night, one of the other waiters hasn't come to work, and you have more tables than usual to wait on. You are weighed down with plates and all the customers are complaining about their food. The chef is yelling at you to clean up a mess you made when you dropped a dish. On top of everything else, your suspenders are broken, and your pants keep falling down while you work. The floor is wet, and you keep slipping as you struggle to meet your responsibilities.

More Scenes

Now create some imaginary conditions for yourself as a character in the following situations. Select circumstances which will add humor to the situation, and then pantomime a short scene in the situation you've created.

☆ You're a wire walker on the opening night of the circus.
☆ You're a teacher on the first day of class.
☆ You're a policeman, breaking up a fight.

6

how to
get what
you want

how to get what you want

As a clown you must motivate your actions. This makes your character believable and integrates your actions into your clown character. After a lot of practice and experience, you may be able to perform your clown character instinctively, but at least in the beginning, it's important to think about and plan *why* your character does what he or she does. Consider these questions:

What does your character want?
What will he or she do to get it?

What Do I Want?

Your character should have a motivating force—one basic need which drives your character into action.

☆ You want to be loved—
☆ You want to be accepted—
☆ You always want to eat—
☆ You want a lot of money—
☆ You want fame—
☆ You want to do a good job.

Your motivating force is your character's main reason for living. State it in a way which will spur you to action—interesting, funny action. Instead of saying, "I want fame," for example, it might be more interesting to say, "I want to look like a movie star." Instead of saying, "I want to be loved," it might be more interesting to say, "I want to be irresistible to the opposite sex."

Experiment with different motivating forces until you find one which fits the image and character of your clown and is geared to the type of routine you want to do. Contradictions often work very well. For instance, let's say your clown is a real idiot. It might be funny if his motivation was "to understand everything completely," or "to let the world know how smart I am." Maybe your clown is a freaky woman who wants to "find the man of my dreams," or "look like a glamorous celebrity."

*Clowns traditionally
tease the ringmaster.*

Trial and error is the key to finding out what makes your character tick and how he or she might be funny.

Motivating the Referee

Select 3 different motivating forces and introduce the boxing match again, as you did in the last chapter. Do it 3 times, using a different motivating force each time. For example, your motivating force might be that you want to be great and successful, or it might be that you want to get home and go to sleep.

Objectives

An *objective* is what you (your character) want in a particular clown routine. Your objective should fit into—or become a part of—your motivating force. Let's say that your motivating force is that you "want to be successful and famous." As the referee in the boxing match, your objective may be "to make sure the champion wins," because the fight is fixed and you've been promised a promotion and a pay raise if he wins.

If your motivating force is that you "want to go home and go to sleep," then your objective in the boxing match might be to "get the fight over with as quickly as possible."

In every routine, experiment with different objectives.

What Will I Do to Get What I Want?
Actions and Activities

So far you've thought about what you want and why. Your *actions* and *activities* will get you what you want. An *action* tells how you're going to go about getting what you want, or how you plan to achieve your objective. For instance, in the boxing match, if your objective is to "make sure the champion wins," some of your actions could be to *"help* the champ stay on his feet," to *"psych out* the challenger," to *"favor* the champ in close calls," or to *"instill confidence* in the champ."

Activities are sub-actions, or specific things you do to carry out your actions. If your action is to instill confidence in the champ, some of your activities may be: smile at the champ a lot, pat the champ on the back, convince the champ he looks great, or give the champ a terrific introduction to the crowd.

If your action is to psych out the challenger, then some of your activities might be: give the challenger dirty looks, convince him he's sick, accuse him of cheating and low blows, or pull his chair away when he goes to his corner to sit down.

It's important to view clown routines as a series of connected actions and activities which your character must perform. In some clown routines and skits, you'll have a choice of many different actions and a variety of activities to achieve your objective. By improvising (more about improvising later in this chapter) and through trial and error, you should select actions and activities which feel right for your character and which will help you get laughs or any other response you want from the audience.

Your activities, as a clown, should have a light and comic tone or quality. If you pull the challenger's chair away, as suggested above, do it in a jestful and cute way, not viciously and maliciously. Look at the following sequence of a clown walking, tripping, falling and getting up. Then look at the same sequence (below) with a different ending. The second sequence is more appropriate for a clown, because it ends with the clown letting the audience know he's okay. This allows the audience to laugh.

If you look as though you're really injured, you may frighten and alienate your audience.

Violence among clowns should be funny, not tragic.

54

Two characters with the same motivating forces will do different things to get what they want. For instance, one character who wants love might sacrifice career, pride or health for it, while another might want love, but be unwilling to sacrifice *anything* for it. Clowns exaggerate human behavior, so you can go to crazy, absurd or outrageous extremes to get what you want.

On the other hand, if you're a very simple clown, your repertoire of actions and activities might be severely limited: you might cry every time you can't get what you want, for example.

Some clowns would chop off the ringmaster's head for a cherry lollipop.

Beats

It's useful to divide up clown routines into smaller sections called *beats*. A beat is a section of a routine which groups a series of activities together in some way. You can divide the boxing match into these beats:

1. Introduction of the fight and the boxers
2. Round 1
3. Round 2
4. Round 3
5. The Exit

You can divide a routine into beats in many ways. There is no set formula for it. Simply create small sections of the routine so that you can concentrate on just one part at a time. It helps if you can identify one major action for each beat. Then you'll have activities in the beat which will help you accomplish your action.

Let's take a look at Beat 1, the introduction of the fight, and assume you're the referee. Imagine that your motivating force is to "appear successful." Your objective in the routine is to "get that woman (or man) I'm dating (in the audience) to marry me." Your action in Beat 1 is to impress your friend with the control and power you have in the ring.

Here are some activities you might perform to help achieve your action and objective:

☆ Slowly enter the ring at the beginning of the routine, walking as if you were a king or queen.
☆ Snap your fingers for the microphone, so you can introduce the fight.
☆ Wink at the reporter in the first row as if he or she were your buddy.
☆ Ruthlessly boss the champion around when you introduce him: slap him on the back, kick him in the butt, order him to tuck in his shirt.
☆ Make the challenger light your cigar.

Let's look at another example. Imagine you're the challenger in the fight. You're a tall, thin, meek character who is not very bright. Your motivating force is "to be loved and admired." Your objective is "to win the match," because your manager promised you a present if you win. The beat is Round 1 and your main action in it is to "follow the referee's orders so that I don't make a mistake." Figure out some activities you might perform in this beat.

Improvisations

When you improvise, you act out a routine or part of a routine spontaneously. You perform actions and activities as they pop into your head. You can improvise about a character, a theme, or you might decide upon specific actions or situations in advance and improvise the rest. In Chapter 3 you improvised making an entrance, saying "hello," and making an exit. Now try these improvisations:

1. Imagine that you're a mad scientist in your laboratory. (You can use kitchen utensils and jars or glasses of water as your equipment.) You are testing a theory you've been working on for 3 years. Decide on a motivating force for the character and an objective. Improvise some actions and activities to create a funny scene.

2. Imagine you're an old man or an old woman sitting on a park bench. Decide on a motivating force and objective for this character. Improvise your actions and activities.

For Two or More Actors

3. Improvise a scene in a waiting room of a dentist's office. Each character should have a different motivating force and objective. Exaggerate your actions and activities to create a comical situation. For example, one patient might panic when the nurse calls his name, and hide behind his chair. The dentist could run into the room to get the patient with a big hammer and chisel.

4. Fill a sack or a box with hats. Each person in the group should reach into the box, select a hat at random, and immediately assume a clown character to go with the hat. Create a 3–5 minute improvisation together using these characters. As you improvise, be sure to establish:

where you are—

why you're there—

what you're trying to accomplish.

Later in the book you'll be working on more complicated clown routines. Break down each routine into a series of beats. Decide on the objective for your character and experiment with different actions and activities. Remember that *how* and *why* you perform your actions are as important as what you actually do. Every action and activity should be part of an attempt to satisfy your character's motivating force and objective. Work on one beat at a time, when you want to polish your routine.

7
the secret thoughts of your clown

the secret thoughts of your clown

It's important to maintain your character throughout a routine. Every moment you're on stage you should be concentrating on what your character would be concentrating on. This will reduce any "awkward feeling" on stage, help you deal with stage fright, and make your character more real to the audience, as well as to yourself. As a clown you can concentrate on:

☆ your actions—
☆ other clowns or the audience—
☆ objects or props—
☆ your inner thoughts, as the character.

Concentrating on Actions

Many times you'll have to invent stage business or activities to keep your character occupied. For instance, if you're waiting for

another clown to enter, you might make believe it's very hot and fan yourself, comb your hair, tuck in your shirt, sing to yourself—the possibilities are endless. Select activities which your character might do, activities that fit into his or her actions and objective, activities which are funny.

If your action in a routine is to make someone notice you, then concentrate on that until you achieve it—or until your action changes.

The female clown is giving the focus to the male clown. She is looking, listening, and observing.

59

Concentrating on Other Clowns or the Audience

There are times in a routine when your partner should have the attention of the audience, times when you need to be passive and observe and receive information from your surroundings. The trick here is to genuinely observe—really to look and listen, understand and react with your actions. It's a mistake to be so busy "acting" that you don't take the time to observe.

The male clown is giving the focus to the female clown.

Concentrating on Objects and Props

When you're a clown, your props become extensions of your character. Play with your props as you rehearse, until you find ways to handle them which are comfortable for your character and your activities. These objects often become the center of attention (Remember the ways you used your hat? See page 16), and you can focus your thoughts on them. Clowns often use props in unconventional ways, as in the classic situation of the clown dancing with a broom. Observe your props, play with them, react to them, and never ever take them for granted.

Select an object from around your house. Improvise with it, using it in many different ways, ways in which it was never intended to be used. For example, use a shoe to comb your hair—and as a pillow.

Work out a short skit in which you make an entrance, say "hello," use your object in at least 3 different ways and make an exit. Then pick another object and do the same thing with a partner.

Concentrating on Your Inner Thoughts

Even if you're not concentrating on your actions, props or other characters, you should still be thinking in character. You need to learn to talk to yourself on stage. You can talk about another clown, about your actions, about what you want; you can react to events and conversation in the routine, sing to yourself, or think of anything which relates to your character's needs and objectives. You can even mumble obscenities to yourself—no one will know. If it makes you funnier, then do it.

Before you begin work on your character, know your motivating force and objective. Your concentration and thoughts will go from one thing to another, but be aware of what you are thinking of or concentrating on. Make sure you're focused at every moment on either your actions or objectives, an object or prop, another clown or member of the audience (possibly imaginary), or your thoughts, as your character would think.

8
discover your clown

discover your clown

It's time to make some temporary decisions about who your clown is. As you work on the clown routines and explorations in this chapter, you can reshape and change your clown or add new dimensions to it. It's important not to be too rigid when you first start performing a clown character. Let it evolve slowly and blossom from something inside you over a period of time.

Before you go on reading, make a tentative decision about:

1. The type of clown you want to portray

    ☆ Auguste
    ☆ Whiteface
    ☆ Character
    ☆ A combination of the above

2. Your clown image

    ☆ Costume
    ☆ Makeup
    ☆ General feeling of character

You don't have to wear a costume and makeup at this point. You can work on that later. But you might want to draw pictures of the character and start rehearsing using elements of costumes, especially your hat.

3. A biography of your clown

4. A motivating force

5. A clown walk and some characteristic movements and mannerisms

6. A clown voice—if you want to use one

7. A theme song for your clown.

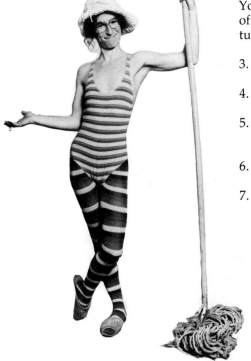

You can rehearse with a suggestion of a costume to help you create your character. It's useful to work with hats, gloves, shoes and hand props—such as this mop.

Some Tips

When it comes to developing your clown, whatever works is right. Trial and error is standard procedure in comedy. Ask yourself, "How does this feel?" "Does it feel right?" When you start to work in front of an audience, you'll be able to get some feedback. You'll discover what people laugh at, when they laugh, and if you're lucky, why they laugh.

Use the exercises in the preceding chapters as a guide. Take the work seriously, but don't think too much or intellectualize. Have fun and be spontaneous. The more you rehearse your actions and the more you know what you're doing—or trying to do—the easier it will be to play and experiment with the clown routines in the next part of this book.

Don't play for laughs. Play your character and his or her actions. You want people to laugh at your clown character, not at you as a person. Be bigger than life by stylizing your movements. Remember that you want to entertain and enlighten the audience, not intimidate or confuse them.

If the audience looks like this when you perform, you're on the right track.

If the audience looks like this, you're doing something wrong.

See as many silent movie comedies as possible, especially the films of Charlie Chaplin, Buster Keaton, Laurel and Hardy and Harold Lloyd—also the Marx Brothers, W. C. Fields and Peter Sellers.

Keep a notebook for your character and comedy ideas.

Your Clown in Different Situations

You'll be the same clown character in many different situations, so you need to adapt your character to the role you're playing. Improvise as the *same* clown in the following situations, and then create a short skit about each one. Be very clear about your motivating force, objective and immediate circumstances, and rehearse your actions so that you know them well. Be especially careful to create the inner life and thoughts of your clown. Concentrate, as you did in the last chapter, and have fun!

☆ You're a clown fireman putting out a small fire.
☆ You're a clown doctor, examining an obese female patient.
☆ You're a clown dogcatcher whose dogs have escaped.

9
the whipcracker

the whipcracker

You'll need one or two partners to perform most of the routines that follow. Performing solo is very difficult for a clown, especially for a beginner. It helps to have a partner to work with, and it's easier to create comedy with more than one person in a routine.

The Whipcracker is a simple clown routine for two performers: a master whipcracker and his stupid assistant. Use the clown characters which you're developing and apply them to the roles and circumstances of the routine. You might also want to experiment with the whiteface-auguste relationship (see page 36). Studying "The Whipcracker" will also teach you more about staging, focus, selling a routine and comic timing. But before you learn "The Whipcracker," try playing a theatre game called "Please—No." It will develop a performing relationship between you and your partner.

Please—No

Most dramatic and comic scenes involving two characters have a "please—no" structure. This means that one character (represented by *please*) wants something from another, but the other character (represented by *no*) will not or cannot give what the first one wants. "Please—No" is an improvisation in which you must follow these rules:

Clown #1 is *please*, and all that he or she can say is the word *please*.

Clown #2 is *no*, and all that he or she can say is the word *no*.

Clown #1's objective is to make Clown #2 say "yes" or "All right."

Clown #2's objective is to keep saying "no" and not give in to Clown #1.

Clown #1 initiates the action by saying "please" and by physically touching Clown #2 (with any part of the body).

Clown #2 responds by saying "no" and by physically moving away.

Play this game until you've exhausted all the possible ways to interact, that is, to say "please" and "no." Then switch roles and play the game again. Take time to listen and respond to your partner and allow yourself to be spontaneous. Concentrate on your objective and don't think too much. When you work on the Whipcracker routine, decide which character is like the *please* and which is like the *no*.

The Whipcracker

Characters: The Whipcracker
                     The Stupid Assistant

Props: A whip (use a small toy whip or simply tie a rope to a stick)
           One sheet of newspaper
           A mirror
           A blindfold or scarf

Often in circuses and variety shows there is a classic act in which a highly skilled whip handler displays his mastery and accuracy. He uses an assistant, as a knife thrower does, and whips objects dangerously close to the assistant. "The Whipcracker," as a clown routine, is a satire of that act. It goes like this:

The whipcracker and the assistant make a brisk, high-energy entrance and take a bow. The whipcracker is holding a whip, a blindfold and a prop mirror.

After the bow or introduction, the whipcracker goes to his place to prepare to crack his whip at the sheet of newspaper which the assistant will present. The assistant, unbeknown to the whipcracker, follows directly behind him and ends up standing where the whipcracker cannot see her.

The whipcracker looks across the stage for the assistant, but to his surprise no one is there.

Slowly he realizes that the assistant is behind him.

He turns to the assistant—grabs her by the collar, and drags her across the stage to her proper position, indicating clearly where she should stand.

Again, the whipcracker crosses the stage to his place. Again the assistant follows and ends up in the same position.

The whipcracker looks for the assistant, and of course she is not there. He realizes (this time more quickly) that the assistant is behind him,

and again he drags her back to the proper position (in the same way he did it the first time).

The whipcracker then goes to his place, and for the third time the assistant follows and ends up behind him. The whipcracker looks across the stage for the assistant again and, again, and she is not there. He immediately realizes what has happened and gets very angry. He does a *slow burn* and a *take* to the audience. Then the assistant—in fear of the whipcracker—pulls herself up by the collar and drags herself to her proper position, where she acknowledges the whipcracker and awaits his next command.

Takes and Slow Burns

Clowns often do *takes* to the audience. It's a *take* when a clown reacts to something with a frozen attitude or facial expression. Usually a clown does a take when he or she perceives something unusual or surprising, like a foe with a shotgun, a beautiful woman, a loud noise, a peculiar object or prop. Clowns often direct their takes to the audience, as if it were a good friend. You can direct a take to the entire audience or to an individual in the audience. When you do a take, you should be saying (silently) to yourself a short sentence or phrase like, "What the heck was that?" or "I can't believe it!" or "I'll get that guy!"

A *slow burn* is a take in which a clown slowly expresses that he is about to burst open or burn up with rage.

The whipcracker pulls out his whip as the assistant opens the newspaper. The whipcracker counts to 3 as he prepares to split the newspaper in half. The assistant holds the paper out, obviously terrified.

71

The whipcracker snaps the whip in the direction of the newspaper. As he does it, the assistant rips the paper in two, which makes it seem as though the whipcracker has actually split the paper.

They marvel at the feat and take a big bow. If you time it right, you can create the illusion that the whipcracker has actually split the paper. But the people in the audience know all the while that this is a gimmick, and that the clowns are trying to fake them out.

For his second trick, the whipcracker holds up his mirror and cracks the whip at the remaining newspaper with his back turned, again on a 3-count.

This time there is a short delay from the time the whipcracker snaps the whip to the time when the assistant rips the paper in two. This delay, if timed just right, should get a laugh, since it exposes the clowns' gimmick. They awkwardly bow and try to cover up the mistake. The whipcracker is holding back his anger with great effort.

For his third and last trick, the whipcracker announces that he will attempt to split the paper while blindfolded. He puts on the blindfold. The assistant is more terrified than ever and shakes all over. The whipcracker snaps the whip.

The assistant is so afraid and frantic that she nervously keeps tearing the paper in half and then into little pieces.

The whipcracker is beside himself with anger. He ominously approaches the assistant and stands next to her as she continues to tear the paper into little pieces.

This completely undoes the whipcracker's gimmick by exposing it to the audience.

The assistant finally realizes what she is doing, stops, shyly looks at the whipcracker as if to apologize, and then throws all the little pieces of newspaper into the furious whipcracker's face.

There is a deadly pause, and then the whipcracker chases the assistant off-stage, which ends the routine.

Staging and Focus

Make sure your gestures are big, clear and exaggerated. Every one of them should be seen by the audience. Practice handling your props so that the audience can see clearly what you're doing. Be particularly aware of whom you're playing to. Are you relating to your partner, for instance, the audience, your prop, yourself? Or some combination of the above? No matter what you're relating to, you want your audience to see and understand the action.

Decide where you want the audience to look at any given moment in the routine. For example, when you want the audience to focus on the whipcracker, the assistant should be relatively still or also watching the whipcracker. It's all too easy for one character to steal the attention of the audience—accidentally or unconsciously—or dominate its attention. In the theatre, this stealing of attention is called *upstaging*. (See page 60, about listening and observing.)

Timing

Timing refers to the speed and rhythm of your actions and reactions. For example, before you lose your temper, you might pause for what seems like a long time, and then suddenly explode with an exaggerated angry reaction. Or you might time your movements with your partner so that you're exactly synchronized. This could be particularly useful when the assistant follows the whipcracker to his position.

You can't learn comic timing from a book. The right timing comes from exploring all kinds of possibilities and trying things out in front of an audience. If audiences laugh at the places where you want them to laugh, then your timing is correct. Some people have an instinctive sense of comic timing; others have to work hard to achieve it.

A good way to learn comic timing is to study silent comedy films, particularly those of Chaplin, Keaton, and Laurel and Hardy.

Selling the Routine

"Selling the routine" means making it work—making it entertaining to the audience. Your routine should never drag or become awkwardly slow. There should never be a dull, uninteresting moment in your act.

One way to sell "The Whipcracker" is to be enthusiastic and energetic throughout. Another way is to stay in character. Know your objective, stick to it, and always find something to do, think, express, or sense, which you can relate to your character's objective and actions.

Perhaps the whipcracker's objective is to impress the critics, while the assistant's objective is to have fun because she is bored.

Other Possibilities

After you've learned the routine, experiment with it. Try different objectives or different actions. For example, the whipcracker might attempt some other tricks, or you might change the relationship between the whipcracker and the assistant.

Experiment with creating your own routine with similar characters in a similar situation: a sharpshooter and assistant, a knife thrower and assistant (see page 136), or a magician and assistant. More about creating your own routines in Chapter 15.

10
the boxing gag

the boxing gag

Here is another classic clown routine called "The Boxing Gag." It requires 3 clowns: a referee and 2 boxers. To perform the routine, you need to learn some of the basic skills of slapstick: how to hit another clown and how to take a slap and fall down.

Slapstick

Slapstick is an essential part of Clown. It's an exaggerated satirical form of comedy in which clowns use the illusion of physical violence and destruction in dealing with other clowns, objects, situations or themselves. But don't confuse this violence and destruction with realistic or tragic theatrical violence. The results of slapstick are comedy, laughter and a light-hearted release of tension (see page 54). The "violence" is poetic, and the audience is always aware that no one is really hurt. It's like the violence in cartoons. If it's done properly, it serves the development of the plot, characters and comedy in a routine.

Giving and Taking a Slap

Stand facing your partner, about an arm's length apart, as shown.

Decide who will give the slap and who will take it. Slap your partner using your downstage arm—the arm that is closest to the audience. (Even though you're not on stage, always decide where the "audience" is, whenever you rehearse.) Your hand should just reach your partner's face when your arm is extended.

Swing your arm slowly, as if you're going to slap your partner, but stop just before you make contact with his or her face. Do this many times slowly, so that you can learn where to stop your swing and so that your partner learns to trust that you won't really make contact.

The clown who is getting slapped should clap his hands and throw his head abruptly to the side in the upstage direction—or away from the hand that is slapping. This staccato movement of the head gives the illusion of impact. If you clap your hands exactly when the slapper's hand arrives, it will look and sound as though you've really been hit.

Make sure you clap your hands at waist level, and try not to make them a focus of attention. If you and your partner can draw people's attention to your faces, they won't notice the hands clapping, and the illusion will work better.

Clap here *Not here*

Reverse roles and keep practicing the slaps until you can do them easily and naturally. Try the same thing with the "slap-ee" facing the audience.

Now improvise an argument which leads to an exchange of slaps.

Falling

Always practice falling on a gym mat, rug or other cushioned surface. Before you start falling, you need to stretch and warm up your body so that you don't hurt yourself. It's a good idea to warm up before *every* rehearsal. See page 152 for a warmup routine.

Here are 3 stylized clown falls:

Fall #1—Both legs straight

Bend your legs (illus. 1 and 2) as if you're going to sit on the floor. Roll on your buttocks and back and slap the mat with both hands. When you slap the mat, you create the sound of falling and, at the same time, break your fall. Use the slap to roll forward into the final stylized, sitting position (illus. 3).

Fall #2—One leg straight

The procedure is exactly the same as before, but this time, fall back with one leg straight and one bent.

Fall #3—Trip and fall

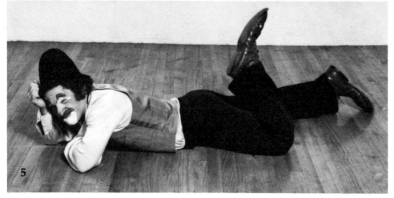

Catch your right foot behind your left ankle while walking and trip on yourself (illus. 3). Now trip and fall forward. Break your fall with your hands and arms and make sure you protect your face. Slap the mat with your hands and allow your arms to absorb the shock of the impact by bending, as though you're doing a pushup on the way down. Finally, let the audience know you're all right.

Other slaps, blows and falls

Here are some other techniques for destruction, which may give you ideas for inventing your own.

Remember: all your slaps and falls should have a comic feeling, and you always need to let the audience know that you haven't been hurt.

When you do a fall, always land facing the audience, if possible. If you want to land in profile, or at an angle to the audience, make sure you let the audience see your face and your reaction.

Practice the slaps and falls until you can do them easily, naturally and instinctively, and so that you don't look as though you're afraid of getting hurt. The more habitual your skills, the more you'll be able to concentrate on your character and your actions.

Now combine the slaps with the falls. Take a slap and use the momentum of the blow to fall. Get up and hit your partner; he or she falls.

Next, work out a short fighting sequence with an exchange of slaps and falls. Again improvise the argument which leads to the fight.

Staying in Character

It's important to perform your slaps and falls as your character would do them. One character might get angry after a fall. Another might cry or laugh. One clown might get up slowly; another might jump right back up to his feet. Your slapstick skills should not stand out awkwardly apart from your character.

Try the following scenes with your clown character, making sure you stay in character throughout:

1. Imagine you see another clown on the other side of the stage. He is leaving. You wave at him and call him, but he doesn't hear you. You start to run after him. Think of a specific important reason why you *must* catch the other clown before he leaves. You run a few steps and suddenly trip and fall. Look to see what you tripped on. React to the audience and then continue your pursuit.

2. Create another fight scene with your partner, using slaps and falls. Concentrate on maintaining your character throughout the fight.

The Boxing Gag

Characters: The Referee
2 Boxers

Props: Slap boxing gloves
Bell or horn
2 stools or milk crates
Towel

You can rehearse and perform this routine without slap boxing gloves, but it works best with them.

Making Slap Boxing Gloves

NEEDED FOR SLAP BOXING GLOVES:

1½ yards (135 cm) of vinyl material
A 4′ × 2′ (120 × 60 cm) piece of cardboard or masonite
2 long sneaker laces
Hole punch

Cut these shapes from a vinyl material—2 pieces for your right hand, 2 for your left. Make a slit in the 2 palm-side pieces and put holes in them with a hole punch. You'll be using a long sneaker lace to thread the glove on your hand so it doesn't fall off.

Two Halves of Right Glove

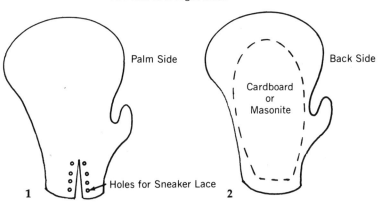

Palm Side

Back Side

Cardboard or Masonite

Holes for Sneaker Lace

1   2

Cut a piece of cardboard or masonite to fit inside the glove (illus. 2). That stiffener will make a loud popping sound when you slap your gloves together.

Sew the glove halves together, with the cardboard or masonite in between, and thread the holes with the long sneaker lace. Place your hand in the glove with your palm behind the cardboard. Secure the glove (illus. 3).

3

The gloves create a comic effect. Practice giving and taking slaps with them so they pop loudly every time you clap them together.

The Routine

The referee makes an entrance. He has a bell, horn or whistle which starts and ends each round and a towel for fanning the boxers. He introduces the fight and then announces the first boxer, who makes her entrance with her stool.

The first boxer is the champion, a big, hulky, tough and fearless brute. She introduces herself to the audience and takes her seat.

Next the referee introduces the second boxer, the challenger, who is meek and terrified. She shyly introduces herself to the audience and goes to her corner.

The referee calls the boxers to the center of the ring and explains the rules with the proverbial "there will be none of this."

The referee uses the challenger to demonstrate what is not allowed, striking her in illegal ways and places.

The poor challenger stumbles back to her corner, already woozy. The champ confidently saunters back to her corner. The referee rings his bell and announces Round 1.

The champ agressively slaps the challenger twice. On the third slap, the champ knocks the challenger down.

The challenger slowly gets up and runs behind her stool to hide. The champ chases her around the stool. Just as the champ is about to hit the challenger again, the referee rings the bell to end the round.

After a short rest, the referee starts Round 2. Immediately, the challenger runs up to the champ and slaps her. The champ quickly retaliates and knocks the challenger down. The challenger slowly gets up.

Just as the champ is about to strike again, the challenger points out a fly,

and they both watch it buzz around. The challenger is trying to distract the champ with the fly.

Finally the champ slaps the fly and they watch it fall. The champ gloats over killing the fly.

The challenger takes this opportunity to land a slap. She knocks the champ down.

The champ is furious and gets right up.

Again she chases the challenger to her corner and around the stool.

Just as the champ is about to strike, the referee ends Round 2.

The champ furiously goes back to her corner and the challenger, relieved, collapses on her stool.

After a short rest, the referee begins Round 3, the final round. The 2 fighters come out taking slow, determined steps towards each other as if they were gunfighters.

As soon as they reach striking distance, they pause and quickly break into a tango. They dance across the stage and back 2 or 3 times.

Then the challenger turns the champ around as part of the dance,

swiftly lands a slap, and knocks the champ down.

The champ gets up slowly and swings at the challenger, who ducks.

But the champ hits her after she spins around, following through on the slap.

The challenger gets right up and swings. The champ ducks, and the challenger accidentally knocks out the referee.

The fighters are astonished. They check the referee and try to revive him, but he is out cold.

They awkwardly try to figure out what to do next. Finally they shake hands and carry the referee off-stage together.

Rehearse until you can perform this routine smoothly. You'll need to fill in many of the details, "takes" to the audience and timing, for instance. Switch roles, after you master the skit, and finally, create a boxing routine of your own. Plan on 3 rounds with 3 or 4 slaps and/or falls per round. This will make the act long enough to develop the conflict, but short enough for a quick-paced routine. Three is a good number for comedy. The assistant follows the whipcracker 3 times, you'll notice; and the whipcracker does 3 tricks. Patterns of 3 work well in Clown. Most professionals take this into account when they create their material.

In your own routine, you can change the characters and their relationships and perhaps end the routine differently. For example, the champ might be a little, skinny bully and the challenger a tall, husky, shy character. The referee and the champ might conspire against the challenger, so that the challenger takes a real beating. A good ending for this match would be to have the challenger accidentally knock out the champ and referee in one blow.

Sometimes the boxing routine is performed with 5 clowns. The 2 other clowns act as assistants to the boxers. They take care of their fighters, get into the fight, and add to the humor.

Knocking Authority

Often, in the Boxing Gag, the referee has the hardest time and ends up getting knocked out. In comedy and Clown, authority figures very often get the worst of it. People love to see referees, umpires, cops, schoolteachers, generals, politicians and other disciplinarians abused. It's a common theme in Clown. Remember it when you create your own routines.

11
the levitation gag

the levitation gag

The Levitation Gag is another routine for 3 clowns. The characters are a wizard (or swami) who does the levitating, his assistant, and an innocent passerby.

The Levitation Gag is a good example of a clown routine that's based on a "gimmick." A *gimmick* is a theatrical illusion which clowns create with a special prop. Gimmicks can be very simple—like the tearing of the newspaper in the whipcracker routine and the popping of the gloves in the Boxing Gag—or they can be very complex and difficult to invent, like a clown car that breaks down and does crazy things or like a cook's oven which squirts flames and smoke and finally explodes. In this chapter you'll find out how to construct and operate a clown gimmick called "levitation legs."

As a clown, you must also be an inventor. Most gimmicks cannot be bought in a store. You need to design and construct them yourself so that they "work" in performance. Buster Keaton was a genius at conceptualizing, designing, and constructing clown gimmicks. Almost all the stunts, special props, and crazy effects in his movies he made himself, without using cinematic tricks.

The Levitation Gimmick

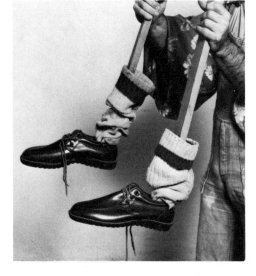

The illusion is that the swami (or levitator) is actually levitating the innocent passerby.

Making Levitation Legs

To make the legs, attach a pair of socks and shoes to the ends of two pieces of light wood—1 × 2's (30 cm × 60 cm) about 3½ to 4 feet (105 cm to 120 cm) long.

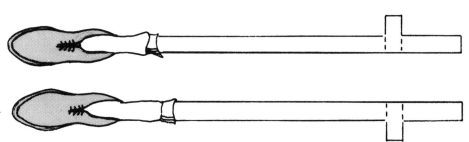

Use carpenter tacks to keep the socks and shoes in place. It helps to add 2 small crossbars for grasping the legs during the routine.

The Bench

You can use a piano bench for this gag, but ideally you should construct a special bench about 4 feet (120 cm) long, with a shelf on one side for storing all the props so you can easily carry them on and off-stage.

Upstage

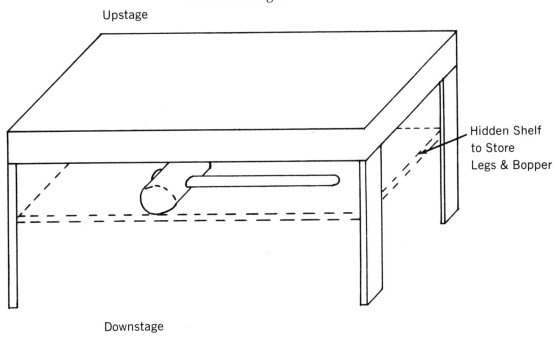

Hidden Shelf
to Store
Legs & Bopper

Downstage

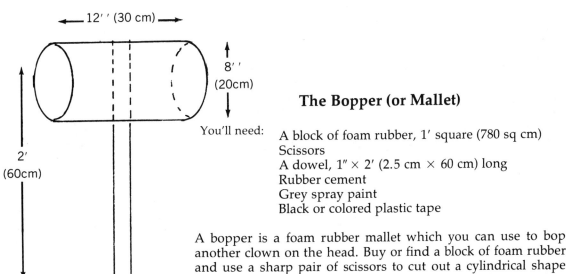

← 12'' (30 cm) →

8''
(20cm)

2'
(60cm)

The Bopper (or Mallet)

You'll need:

A block of foam rubber, 1' square (780 sq cm)
Scissors
A dowel, 1" × 2' (2.5 cm × 60 cm) long
Rubber cement
Grey spray paint
Black or colored plastic tape

A bopper is a foam rubber mallet which you can use to bop another clown on the head. Buy or find a block of foam rubber and use a sharp pair of scissors to cut out a cylindrical shape about 1 foot (30 cm) long and 8 inches (20 cm) in diameter. Use the scissors to pierce a narrow hole across the width of the cylinder. Coat the dowel with rubber cement and insert it into the hole in the foam rubber. This will be the handle of the mallet. Spray the foam rubber with grey paint and decorate the handle with plastic tape.

The Levitation Gag

Characters: Levitator
Assistant
Innocent Passerby

Props: Levitation Legs
Bopper
Bench
Sheet or Blanket (large)

The Routine

The levitator and his assistant make an entrance carrying the bench and props. (If you haven't built the special bench, keep the legs and bopper hidden under the sheet on top of the bench.)

While the levitator takes his bows, the assistant places the legs, the bopper and the sheet on the floor on the upstage side of the bench. (Make sure the legs and bopper are not visible.)

The levitator calls over the assistant and whispers in his ear, gesturing that he needs a volunteer to levitate.

He sends the assistant downstage to look in the audience for a volunteer. The assistant points to someone in the audience and turns to the levitator to confirm his choice.

The levitator shakes his head "no" and pantomimes that the person is too big.

The assistant looks for someone else and finally points to another audience member. He looks to the levitator who pantomimes that the person is too fat.

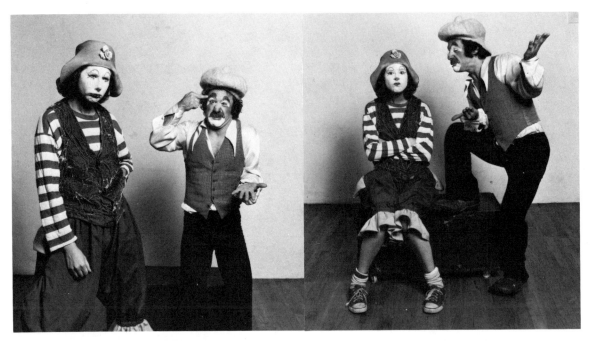

The assistant, annoyed and frustrated, looks again and picks out a third person. He excitedly turns to the levitator, but the levitator arrogantly indicates no, the person looks crazy.

The assistant gets angry and sits on the bench in protest. The levitator runs to the assistant and they argue.

While they're arguing, the third clown—the innocent passerby—makes a brisk entrance, as though going somewhere important.

Both the assistant and the levitator notice her and realize that she is a perfect volunteer. The passerby has no idea what is going on and stands there, bedazzled.

The levitator does a few large hand gestures to hypnotize the volunteer. The last gesture is a sharp, large movement which is supposed to whammy the volunteer.

The assistant and the levitator stare at the volunteer to see if she is in a trance. The volunteer shrugs her shoulders and indicates to the audience that she thinks they're both nuts.

She walks away quickly on her original path. The assistant chases after her and drags her back to center stage. He turns her toward the levitator, who goes through the same

hypnotizing gestures again. Just as the levitator throws the whammy, the disgruntled victim ducks and the assistant gets it. He stiffens up and rocks back and forth as if about to fall over.

The passerby laughs and again starts on her merry way. The assistant snaps out of the trance, immediately runs after the passerby and drags her back for the third time. The passerby is annoyed and angry, but stands by while the levitator goes through his routine again.

This time, as the levitator goes through his motions, the assistant reaches down behind the bench and gets the bopper. He sneaks up, and just as the levitator whammies the passerby, the assistant inconspicuously bops her on the head.

This finally puts the passerby in a trance. She stiffens up and rocks back and forth. The assistant catches her as she falls and puts her down on the bench to be levitated.

The assistant and the levitator reach back for the sheet or blanket and hold it up in front of the bench.

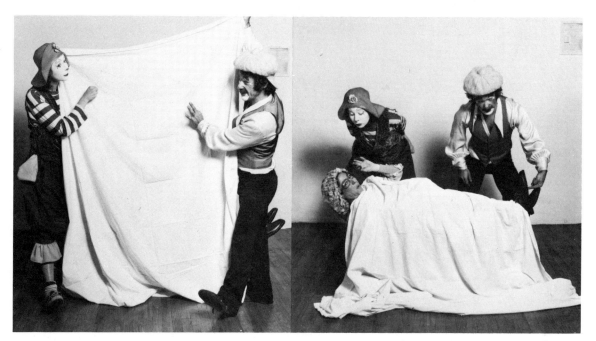

They stall for time by cleaning it off. This gives the passerby time to put the levitation legs in position to replace her own legs. The assistant and the levitator cover the passerby with the blanket which touches the floor. Later, when the passerby is "levitated" and walking around, it must camouflage her real legs. At this point, it should look as though the levitation feet are the passerby's feet. The levitator tickles the phony feet and the passerby giggles. This demonstrates to the audience that the phony levitation legs are connected to the passerby's body.

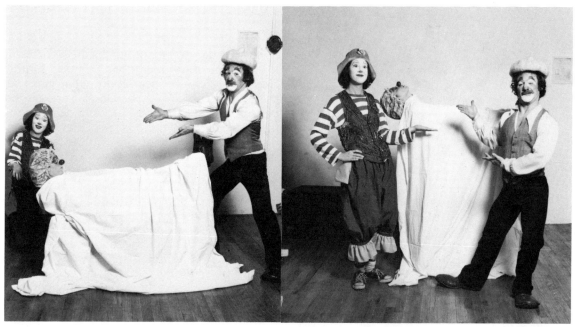

As the levitator makes gestures to levitate the victim, the passerby raises her head and shoulders and lifts the legs a few inches. It looks as though she is starting to rise magically. She falls back down flat and the levitator tries again.

This time she rises even higher before she falls again. The levitator anxiously tries a third time. Now the passerby stands and begins to walk slowly. It should look as if she is floating on air.

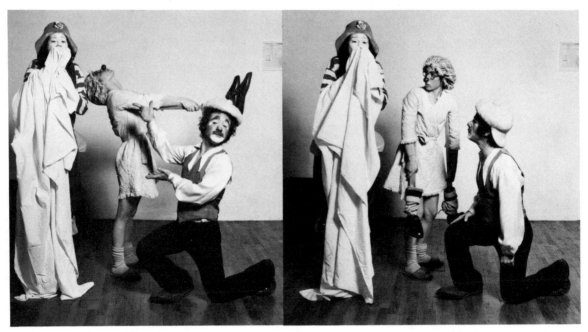

The assistant, who is closely following the whole procedure, has to sneeze. He pulls away the sheet to sneeze on and thereby

reveals the gimmick, making a mockery of the whole routine. The other clowns slowly realize what the assistant has done.

After the initial shock, they angrily chase the assistant off-stage.

Tips on the Levitation Gag

As in all routines, be careful to stay in character, keep the energy going, and sell the routine. Here especially, be clear about what you want the audience to focus on. Don't upstage your partners or distract from the main action. Practice working with the props so that you don't disrupt the rhythm of the routine when you handle them. The business with the legs, for instance, should be smooth and well-rehearsed. The chase at the end should be choreographed carefully. It should punctuate the routine by being very stylized and on a high energy level. Experiment with the rhythm of the routine. Sometimes slow down and even freeze to create a tableau; at other times, move briskly and emphatically. Especially in chases you can juxtapose frantic speedy running against slow moments and freezes in awkward or funny positions.

The Blow-Off

Most clown routines have a *blow-off* or surprise ending. That blow-off is often connected to the gimmick. For instance, the blow-off in the Levitation Gag comes when the assistant pulls the sheet away and reveals the gimmick. In the Boxing Gag the blow-off occurs when the referee is knocked out. The blow-off in The Whipcracker takes place when the assistant throws the little pieces of torn paper in the whipcracker's face.

The blow-off is the termination, culmination or resolution of a conflict which builds during the routine. Blow-offs are usually visual and emphatic, and they may be accompanied by loud sounds or explosions. The blow-off might also be the ultimate blow or degradation of one of the characters, as it is in The Whipcracker. A commonly used blow-off takes place when a clown gets his or her pants or dress torn off by another clown or an animal. This, of course, reveals funny undergarments. Usually a chase and a stylized exit follow the blow-off, and the routine ends.

More about Gimmicks

Gimmicks and blow-offs are important, and many clowns who create their own routines start with an idea for a gimmick or blow-off and build a routine around it. If you have crazy ideas for gimmicks and blow-offs, try them out. You can always find a way to build special props, so don't limit yourself. Give things a chance before you dismiss them as impractical or unfeasible.

Remember, though, that your characters and their relationships are the most important elements in comedy. By all means, use gimmicks and blow-offs in the service of your character, but you can't sit back and expect a good gimmick or a funny blow-off to make you into a good clown. The challenge is to integrate these things meaningfully into your personal style, sense of timing, and ability to project and sell a routine.

The Innocent Victim

The innocent passerby in this routine is a classic "innocent victim," a character often used in comedy and Clown. The innocent victim just happens to be in the wrong place at the wrong time. Consequently, he or she gets abused, slapped around, pies in the face, buckets of water on the head, or worse. As with violence in slapstick, don't confuse the suffering of the innocent victim in comedy with the suffering of the innocent in tragedy.

The exaggeration, absurdity, timing, comic characterization, and style of Clown allows us to laugh at the suffering of the innocent victim. Maybe we're laughing at all the times we suffer, feel helpless, and can't figure out why.

The innocent victim, like the villain in a melodrama, often gets it in the end.

the washerwomen

the washerwomen

The Washerwomen is a routine for 2 clowns, usually 2 men dressed as cleaning ladies. It contains elements of slapstick: absurdity, one-upmanship, stupidity, and exaggeration. Working on this routine will help you develop skill in building a conflict from a personality clash and small slapstick exchanges to an absurd and extreme exchange of destruction. Laurel and Hardy were masters at building such conflicts. The conflict is tied into the idea of competition and one-upmanship:

☆ Clown #1 does something, usually destructive.
☆ Clown #2 tries to outdo Clown #1 by doing something similar but more emphatic, larger, more exaggerated.
☆ Clown #1 retaliates with a bigger gesture.
☆ This retaliation continues between the clowns until it builds to a totally absurd and disastrous degree.

In The Washerwomen routine the 2 cleaning ladies come on stage to clean and they end up arguing and fighting and making a total mess of themselves and the stage.

Men in Women's Clothes

Men-dressing-up-like-women is a classic "bit" or comic characterization in Clown. Don't make the mistake of thinking that male clowns dressed as cleaning ladies suggests homosexuality, or that it's a serious comment on male and female roles. There's a good reason why male clowns often dress like women or play stereotyped female roles—it's funny! People laugh at it, and the routine works.

You may want to experiment with different combinations of Velcro® and snaps so that the dress is loose enough to perform in without tearing and for your partner to rip off easily.

Costumes for The Washerwomen

The clowns in this routine should wear special tear-away dresses stuffed with balloons which create big bosoms and big rear ends. Wear funny underwear and wigs—any cheap wig will do. Select a housecoat which is very big for you. Cut the housecoat into halves along the seams, as shown.

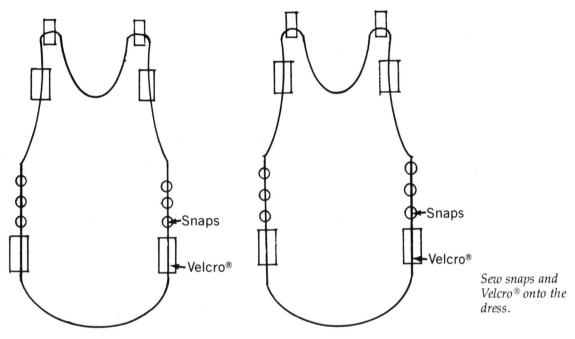

Sew snaps and Velcro® onto the dress.

To attach your balloons, get 2 strings, each about 4 feet (120 cm) long. Tie 2 balloons to each string. Tie 1 set of balloons around your chest and the other around your hips, as shown.

The Washerwomen

Characters: 2 male clowns dressed as cleaning ladies

Props: Washerwomen costumes, with balloons
3 identical buckets
1 mop
2 rags
Confetti or small pieces of torn newspaper
A trick can of peanut brittle or exploding snakes (you
    can buy them at a magic store)
Container of yogurt
Spoon

The Routine

One washerwoman is the boss and the other is the assistant. They enter together, carrying all of their supplies—the buckets, rags, mop, and so on. Two of the buckets should have 1 or 2 quarts of water in them; the third bucket should be about ⅓ full of confetti. All the other props, except for the mop, can be carried on stage inside the bucket.

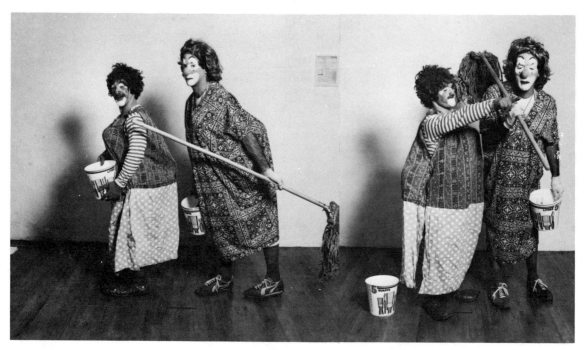

The assistant carries the mop and 2 buckets, and the boss carries the other bucket. After they make a stylized entrance, they put down the buckets. The boss looks around, assesses the situation, and orders the assistant to mop up.

The assistant turns to mop up and accidentally hits the boss in the back of the head with the mop.

The assistant then realizes she has accidentally hit the boss and turns back to apologize.

This slapstick sequence with the mop should be rehearsed very carefully. You must figure out exactly where to stand so that when the assistant turns, the mop will hit the boss in the head. Practice controlling this mop swing, so that you make very light contact with the boss's head. Be careful not to hurt your partner with the mop. The boss should clap her hands (as in the Boxing Gag, see page 78), take the blow by abruptly moving her head forward, and allow the impulse of her head to carry her forward a step.

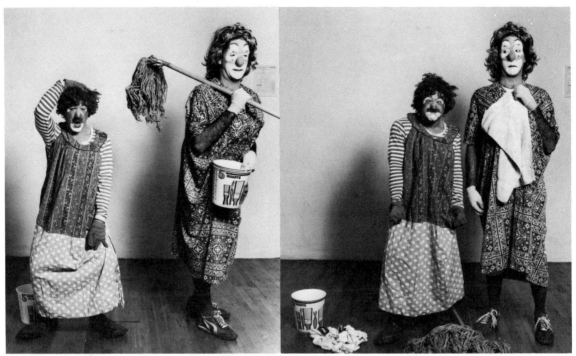

The disgruntled boss yells at the assistant and then orders her to mop up. As the assistant turns again to mop up, she hits the boss again, exactly as she did before.

The assistant realizes she has done something wrong again and freezes. The boss responds to the blow and does a furious take to the audience.

The boss slowly approaches the assistant and taps her on the shoulder. The assistant nervously and shyly turns around to see what the boss wants. The boss angrily gestures that the assistant hit her again. She tells her to be careful and angrily commands her to mop up.

This time the assistant turns very slowly and cautiously, trying not to cause another accident. Sensing that everything is all right, she continues her turn abruptly. The boss wisely senses danger, ducks and avoids another blow.

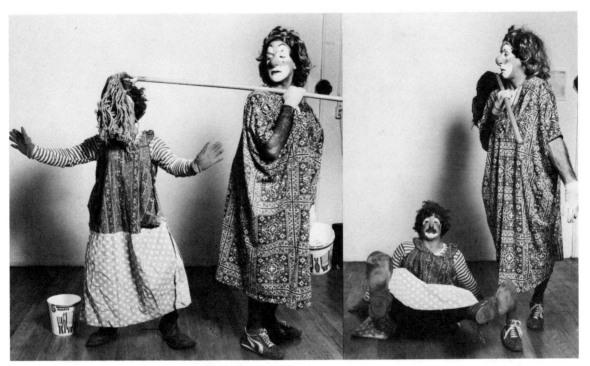

Unfortunately, the assistant turns back to make sure everything is okay. She hits the boss with the mop—in the face, this time— and knocks her down. The assistant rushes to help the boss to her feet, cleans her off, and helps get her together.

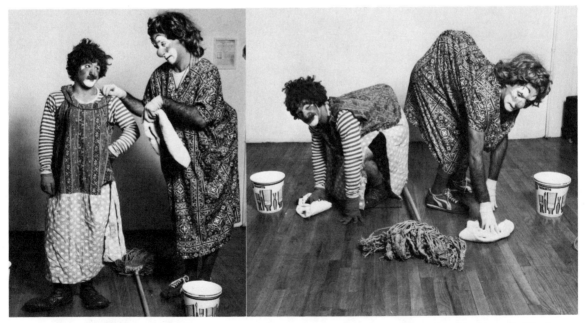

The boss pushes the assistant away, throws the mop to the other end of the stage, slaps the assistant and, for the fourth time, orders the assistant to mop up.

The assistant goes to the mop and begins to work. The boss watches her and then starts to scrub the floor. They sing while they work. After 15–20 seconds, the assistant puts down the mop, and joins the boss at scrubbing the floor.

Suddenly the assistant stops working, yells, "Lunchtime," pulls out a container of yogurt, and begins to enjoy big spoonfuls. The boss, amazed and confused, starts to get angry, but says, "Where's mine?" The assistant hands her a can of peanut brittle.

The boss opens the tin and snakes fly out all over the place (not pictured). The assistant laughs, but the boss is fuming, so the assistant quickly goes back to scrubbing. The boss barely controls her rage, but slowly goes back to scrubbing. Things are calm for a few seconds, until the assistant accidentally hits the boss in the face with her rag.

The assistant continues working, unaware of the accident. The boss glares. The assistant accidentally hits the boss in the face again and soon a third time.

Rage consumes the boss. She slowly and firmly taps the assistant on the shoulder and explains what she has done.

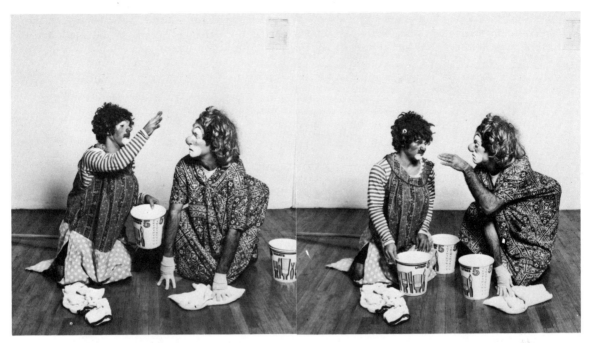

The boss then slowly and with controlled rage throws a handful of water in the assistant's face.

The assistant mimics the boss and retaliates with another handful of water.

The boss vengefully soaks her rag in the water and squeezes it on the assistant's head.

The assistant slowly takes a mouthful of water and spits it in the boss's face.

This sequence of destruction is done with a sense of pride, revenge, competition, one-upmanship, and joy in outdoing each other. But at some point in the conflict, the exchanges become an automatic angry reaction, instead of premeditated vengeance. At that point, the action speeds up.

The boss takes another mouthful of water, twists her own ear, and spits more water in the assistant's face.

The assistant retaliates by pumping water into the boss's face with her arm.

At this point, stage a rapid exchange of spitting and throwing water which builds to the boss dumping her whole pail of water on the assistant's head.

The assistant slowly recovers and retaliates by ripping the boss's dress off.

The boss rips the assistant's dress off.

The assistant slaps the boss who falls down. Her balloons burst on the ground and make a loud noise.

The audience should believe the boss is carrying a pail full of water. (Make sure there are no props in that pail other than the confetti.)

The boss gets up, picks up the pail of confetti and chases the assistant around the stage.

Finally, the boss corners the assistant downstage. The assistant's back is to the audience, and she is downstage of the boss, who is facing the audience.

The audience should now have the feeling that the boss is going to unload a bucket full of water right into their faces.

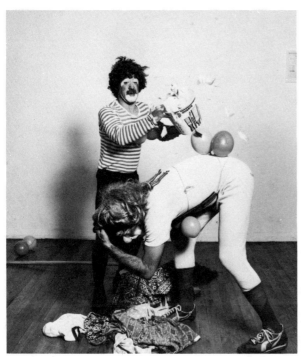

The boss feigns to the left and feigns to the right—with large movements—
and finally unloads the confetti into the audience as the assistant ducks.
The boss quickly chases the assistant off-stage in a stylized exit.

More about One-Upmanship

Often in a routine, as in The Washerwomen, one clown will foul up the plans of another clown. In this routine, the boss wants to clean up, and the assistant acts as a foil to the boss by innocently causing accidents which eventually lead to a fight. In other routines, especially those with a traditional whiteface and auguste clown, one clown rudely and overtly interrupts another clown's solo activities, either accidentally or on purpose, and upstages the clown. This angers the upstaged clown, who generally chases the other clown off-stage and continues the activity, only to be interrupted over and over again. The result is a conflict and a fight.

Improvisations

Improvise in the following situations and experiment with developing an original routine using the one-upmanship theme.

The Painters

Two clowns are hired to paint a luxury apartment or house.

The Concert

One clown attempts to give a musical concert and is continually interrupted by a second clown who keeps coming out to do absurd things.

The Triangle

Two male clowns fight over the affections of a female clown.

After improvising and developing characters for these situations, think of possible blow-offs which you might use to create routines. For instance, in The Concert, if the first clown is playing a violin, perhaps it falls apart at the end of the routine.

13
the wire walker

the wire walker—a solo routine

The Wire Walker is a routine for one clown. It's a satire on a tight-rope or slack rope act in which the clown attempts to walk on a rope which he strings between two chairs. Of course, the chairs keep falling down.

Performing Solo

Performing solo is more difficult than working with a partner because you have no other clown to slap, trick, fight with, outdo, outsmart and develop a comic relationship with. The way you relate to your audience and to your props is therefore more important.

Try to personify your props—that is, give them a personality and develop a relationship with them. For example, your props might not do what you want them to. They might be defective or break, or you might use them improperly. In this way, your props can get in the way of your objective just as your partner would in a conflict. Suppose that you're trying to build a house and your hammer keeps falling apart and all the nails bend like rubber. You finally get the house up—and when you slam the door the whole house falls down!

You can also create a personality for your props by treating them like people: you can love them, get angry at them, or throw them around. Your props might stubbornly resist your attempts to change them, or some props might come to your aid and help you solve a problem. Charlie Chaplin's tramp clown, for instance, uses his cane like a third arm. See Chapter 3, "Discover Your Hat," for more ideas.

When you work alone, it is vital that you develop a strong relationship with the audience. You must win them over, get them to sympathize with you, and charm them into liking you. You can gain their respect by making them laugh, by being sweet, cute and lovable, by performing a difficult skill, like juggling or unicycling, or by portraying your character with perfection. After you make friends with the audience, you can play with them, use them to enhance your routine, and develop a more complex relationship. You can pull people out of the audience and use them on stage as volunteers. You can ask the audience how to solve a problem which you face on stage. You can encourage them to applaud—or boo—when you want; you can go into the audience to perform; you can react emotionally to the audience's responses—laugh with them, get angry at them, or act embarrassed. Most important, you can try to develop a warm sense of sharing with them.

The Wire Walker

Characters: 1 clown who wants to be a wire walker

Props: 2 chairs
20 feet (6 m) of rope
Circus music (taped)

The Routine

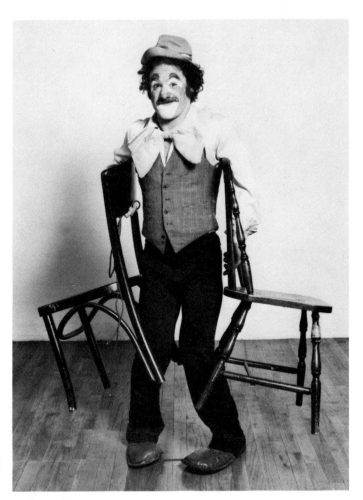

Circus music starts and the clown makes a stylized entrance while carrying 2 chairs and the rope.

The clown sets the chairs down about 10–15 feet (3–5 m) apart and studies them.

He ties one end of the rope to Chair #1 and crosses the stage to tie the other end to Chair #2.

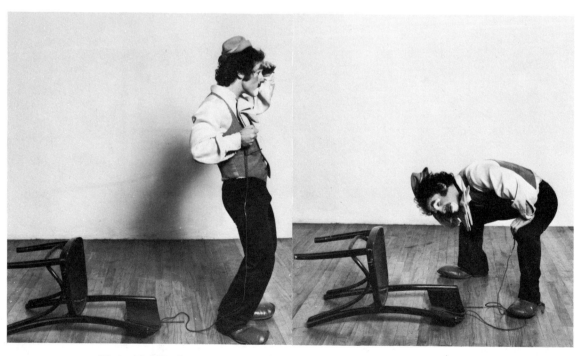

Chair #1 falls down.

He notices that Chair #1 has fallen

and sets it back up again. He crosses to Chair #2, and again Chair #1 is pulled over by the rope,

so he goes back and fixes the chair. The third time he faces Chair #1 as he cautiously moves across the stage and measures the rope, so that the chair doesn't fall. He's satisfied that all is well and quickly turns to Chair #2. This abrupt turn causes Chair #1 to fall again. This time he doesn't notice it.

He ties the rope to Chair #2 and then turns and is amazed that Chair #1 has fallen again.

He quickly runs to fix the chair. When he stands up Chair #1, it causes Chair #2 to fall.

He is again amazed when he discovers Chair #2 is down, and slowly goes to fix it. This causes Chair #1 to fall again.

He then runs to fix Chair #1, and Chair #2 falls. This problem continues and the poor clown runs back and forth, trying to get both chairs to stand up at the same time. Finally he succeeds and he collapses in the middle, exhausted.

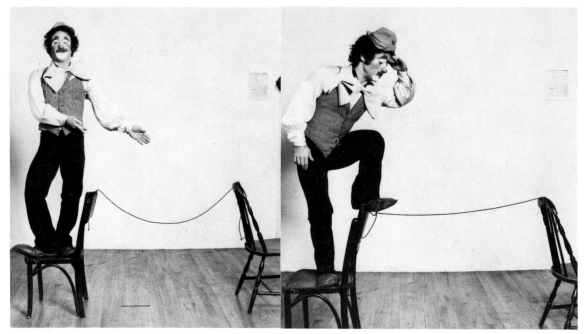

The wire walker slowly gets up, mounts Chair #1, and proudly gestures to his rope, which is strung between the 2 chairs.

He pantomimes to the audience that he is a great wire walker and he is about to walk the rope which he has strung between the chairs.

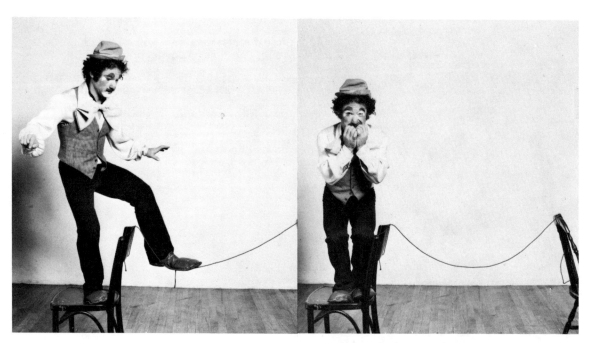

He cautiously places his foot on the rope, and then withdraws it in terror.

He stands on the chair, trembling with fear. Finally, he gathers his courage and tries to walk the rope. Both chairs fall down and he does, too, in a forward roll on the floor. He sits there, baffled.

120

He gets up, assesses the situation, and then gets a brilliant idea. He moves the chairs very close to each other so the rope lies flat on the floor. Now he is ready to achieve this fantastic feat. Again he mounts Chair #1.

Boldly he plunges forward and walks the rope on the ground. He even performs a few brave tricks, like jumping up and down, standing on one foot, and executing quick turns.

Finally, he rushes to Chair #1, mounts it, wipes his brow with relief

and takes a grand bow.

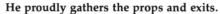
He proudly gathers the props and exits.

Tips on The Wire Walker

This routine is very simple in structure, but it's a difficult routine to sell (see page 75 on selling a routine). Your character must be interesting, charming and funny. It's also important to create the illusion of actually walking the high wire or rope. You must convince the audience that you are 50 feet high, even though you're walking on the ground. Practice the miming of walking a tightrope very carefully and thoroughly. It helps to look down continually and react to your height. Use your imagination to see specific things way down below on the ground, like the tops of people's heads, the ringmaster or an elephant. Creating the details of what you see below will help give you a realistic fear of falling. Try using surprise rhythms when you walk on the wire: suddenly lose your balance, for example, and just as you recover it, lose it again.

Exaggerate your reactions. The way you time those reactions, the timing of the chairs falling, and of your gestures are crucial. You'll need to perform this routine many times before an audience in order to make the timing work.

The routine is absurd, and the contradiction between the clown's fear of heights and the obvious fact that he is really on the ground can make it very funny.

Stupidity and the Clown

Stupidity is a fundamental aspect of clown routines and of the clown's personality. The clown's stupidity is one of the keys to creating comedy and getting laughs. It's funny, because it's an exaggeration of the kinds of mistakes we all make. Often the clown's stupidity is used as a symbol for the imperfection of the human race.

In the Wire Walker, the clown is so simple-minded that he can't figure out how to tie the rope to both chairs without making one fall. He also assumes that the chairs will remain standing when he walks on the rope.

In the Whipcracker, the assistant keeps following the whipcracker, stupidly. The assistant in the Levitation Gag stupidly reveals the gimmick by sneezing into the blanket. In the Washerwomen the stupid assistant keeps hitting the boss in the head with the mop.

Stupidity also allows another fundamental aspect of clowning to emerge—trickery.

Trickery

Because some clown characters are so stupid, it's easy for another clown to fool or trick them. In the Boxing Gag, for example, one of the boxers distracts the other one by pointing to a fly. As the stupid boxer watches the fly, the first boxer slaps him.

In the Washerwomen, the assistant fools the boss with the old exploding-snakes-in-the-can bit; even bosses can be stupid. The one-upmanship and competitive themes in the clown routines (see page 114) also relate to trickery. Clowns often try to outdo, outsmart or outtrick another clown in slapstick conflicts.

Imitation and Mimicry

Imitation and mimicry are also essential to clown routines. Clowns imitate other circus performers and mimic their skills, as in the Wire Walker and the Whipcracker. Clowns mimic each other, too, like the stupid assistant who keeps following the whipcracker. Clowns also mimic and make fun of other people, especially stereotypes like the washerwomen or the referee.

If you're serious about becoming a professional clown, it's important to study Mime. Mime will help you to create characters through your body language. You'll learn to gesture more clearly, develop exaggerated and stylized movement, choreograph your routines, and it will make you more entertaining to watch as you expand your range of body expression.

Discovery

Clowns, especially innocent ones, are forever "discovering" obvious things. The wire walker "discovers" that a chair has fallen. The assistant washerwoman "discovers" she has hit the boss with the mop. The levitator "discovers" the innocent passerby. When you play a routine, look for moments where you can discover something. It may be something very obvious, like the stage, the audience, or that your pants have fallen down. These moments help establish the naiveté and innocence of your character. These are important qualities for a clown, and they are often present in professional clowns. You can get the audience to sympathize and identify with you by pointing up these qualities.

The Mirror Gag—an Exploration into Stupidity, Trickery, Mimicry and Discovery

You may have seen the traditional clown routine called the Mirror Gag in *Duck Soup*, a Marx Brothers movie. It's a routine for 2 clowns (though the Marx Brothers used 3), and an imaginary mirror. If you like, you can build a wooden frame or just make believe there's a mirror there.

Two clowns, dressed exactly the same, *discover* each other through the mirror. One of the clowns is so *stupid* that he does not realize that there is no mirror. He thinks the other clown is his reflection. The other clown *tricks* the stupid clown by *mimicking* everything he does. Slowly, the first clown *discovers* that the other clown is tricking him.

Improvise with a partner in this situation. Be especially aware of stupidity, trickery, mimicry and discovery. If you want to polish the improvisation into a routine, add some slapstick: a slap or slaps, falls, a conflict and a blow-off. Experiment with any crazy ideas that pop into your head.

14
the balloon chase

the balloon chase

The Balloon Chase is a routine for a group or an ensemble of 6–10 clowns. It's lively, exhilarating and a good way to begin a show because the high energy, sound and excitement will grab the audience's attention right away.

A group of mischievous clowns steal balloons from a clown dressed as a balloon vendor who is pretending to sell balloons to the audience. The vendor, trying to recover his balloons, engages the clowns in a wild and crazy chase.

Before you work on the balloon chase, try the theatre game called "Crossovers." It develops timing, mimicry, freedom of expression and spontaneity, as well as group awareness. It's a good game to use whenever you want to help clowns work together in a group. Whenever a number of performers work together, it's important that they become sensitive to each other and learn to work with—and adjust to—the rhythms and styles of the other performers.

Crossovers

Wear comfortable clothing, such as tights and leotards, overalls or shorts. Half the clowns stand at one end of the room and face the other half of the group at the opposite end.

One clown begins the game by moving silently across the room to the opposite line. The crosser should move in a free-form way—any way he or she wants to move. The only requirement is that the clown move in a repetitive pattern, so that everyone in the opposite line can mimic or imitate it in their places. For

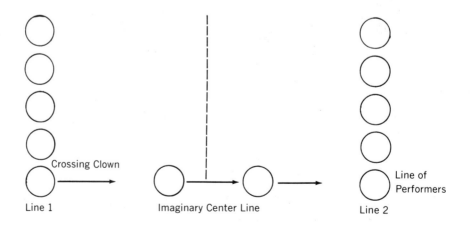

Line 1   Crossing Clown   Imaginary Center Line   Line 2   Line of Performers

instance, the clown might move with shoulders bouncing up and down—or like a gorilla. Anything is acceptable, as long as the pattern is a simple one and the clowns in the other line can mirror the movements.

It's important that the clowns concentrate on becoming exactly like the crosser. The goal is to capture the crosser's essence, spirit and inner life. This is more important than just mimicking the external movements. The clowns can achieve it by carefully observing the crosser's rhythm and attitude. As the crosser approaches the line, he or she should spend a few moments relating to each person on the line, as if communicating or exchanging something. The crosser does this by observing each individual. It's easy to decide quickly and instinctively which person is the best mirror, and the crosser selects that person by establishing eye contact. They slowly change places, and the selected person takes the same movement back across, toward the first line. When this second crosser reaches the imaginary line in the middle of the room or stage—spontaneously, without hesitating or thinking—he or she changes the movement to a new one of his or her own.

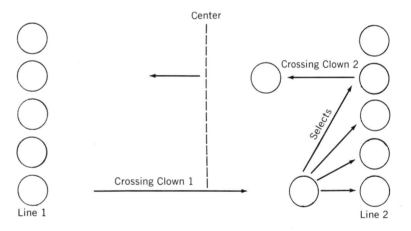

Line #1 now mirrors the second crosser, and the game continues. Each new clown spontaneously changes the movement pattern at the imaginary center line. After 15 or 20 minutes, the director or leader clown should give a signal to indicate that everyone can now make a sound or sounds, or talk along with their movement. The sound is optional, not imperative. End the exercise after 20 to 30 minutes, or when the players stop inventing new movements and patterns.

The goal of this game is not to be funny, but to work closely and sensitively with your partners. It's fun to do, but it's more important to concentrate and follow the rules seriously. There should be no talking or other distractions in the room while the game is being played.

The Gimmick of the Long Shirt
and the Pants Drop

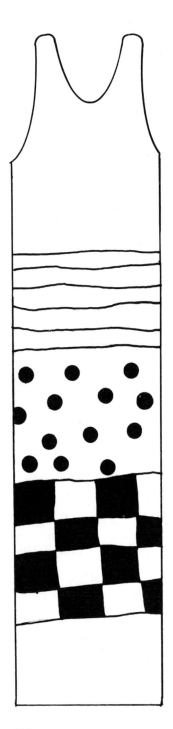

The Balloon Chase ends when the last mischievous clown falls on the balloons while running away from the vendor. The vendor picks him up and then slaps him down. Again he picks him up and pulls off a 20-foot- (6-m-) long shirt and finally the mischievous clown's pants fall down. This reveals his funny underwear, and he runs off in embarrassment.

The Long Shirt

To make a long shirt, use a tank-top-shaped shirt made from strong material.

Add segments of different colorful fabrics to the hem of it, until it is 20 feet (6m) long.

It should look like a long tube. Make sure you reinforce the seams so the shirt can withstand being pulled and tugged. Make it big enough to slip your body into.

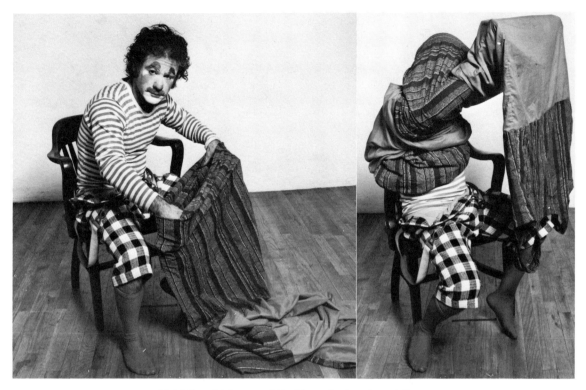

Fold the shirt around itself, as shown, to put it on.

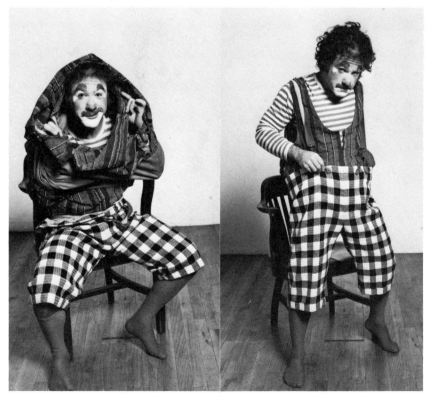

Wear pants that are baggy enough to go over the long shirt. Hold the pants up with suspenders. Slip your arms through the suspenders to make your pants fall down.

129

The Balloon Chase

Characters: Mommy clown
                  Brat Baby clown
                  Balloon vendor
                  3–10 mischievous clowns

Props: Balloons on dowels
          Long shirt
          Mat to fall on

The Routine

This routine works particularly well outdoors—at picnics, track meets, football halftimes—at any event where there is a dispersed focus and lots of space. After you capture everyone's attention with the Balloon Chase, you can follow up with other routines like the Boxing Gag or the Washerwomen.

The clown dressed as a balloon vendor goes through the audience yelling, "Balloons—get your balloons!"

Mommy clown and Brat Baby clown enter. The baby wants a balloon, so Mommy gets one for her.

(It can be very funny if a tall clown plays the baby.)

Meanwhile, 3–10 mischievous clowns conspire to steal the vendor's balloons.

The balloons are stolen, and the vendor chases after them.

The mischievous clowns pass the balloons from one clown to another, and the vendor—as quick as he is—cannot get them.

This chase can go through the audience. Finally, the last clown runs up on stage and trips. He lands on top of the balloons and they burst, making a loud noise.

The vendor catches up to him, picks him up, yells at him, and slaps him. The clown falls. Another clown should inconspicuously place any remaining balloons under his backside, as he falls for the second time.

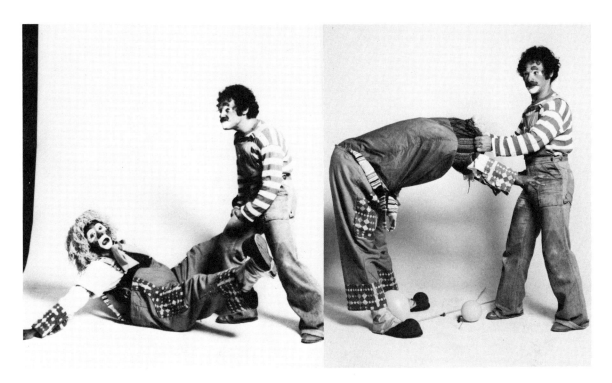

The fallen clown should slip his arms through his suspenders while he is down.

The vendor picks him up and pulls off the long shirt.

Last, the clown's pants fall down. He slowly recovers from the fall, notices his pants are down, picks them up and runs off.

For Groups of Clowns

You can develop many routines for groups of clowns. You might want to try some of these:

1. The Boxing Gag with a referee, 2 boxers, 2 trainers—who help the boxers and get into the fight—and 5 clowns who are part of the audience and get into the match.

2. A baseball game with an umpire, batter, catcher, pitcher and 3 fielders.

3. A birthday party, with funny presents and a pie fight.

15
creating your own routines

creating your own routines

Almost anything is possible in Clown. Clowns reflect things they see in society and the world, and because things change so fast, there are always new ways to express comedy. For example, John McQue, a professional circus clown, is convinced that bugs are slowly taking over the world, so he created a clown routine about it. He carved large bugs out of foam rubber and mounted them on battery-operated police cars. This causes the "bugs" to run around the circus ring, and John, as a clown, battles the bugs with a giant flyswatter, a net and an enormous can of roach spray, which is a decorated fire extinguisher.

In the last few chapters, you've worked on some traditional clown routines. These routines are in the standard repertoire of most professional clowns. When you perform or adapt traditional routines, the challenge is in adding your own personal touches through your unique character and through experimenting with variations in your actions and timing. This is a good way to create your own original material. For instance, you can change the Washerwomen routine into a routine about 2 house painters. The slapstick conflicts and one-upmanship theme can parallel the Washerwomen routine.

The assistant should practice bursting the balloons so he can do it quickly and easily during the routine.

Sometimes you can change the gimmick in a routine, but keep the character relationships and timing. The Whipcracker routine, for instance, can be changed into a knife-thrower act. The knife thrower makes believe he's throwing knives at an assistant, who's leaning against a flat with balloons mounted all around him. Actually, the knife thrower has a toy wooden or rubber knife, and instead of throwing it, he goes through the motions, hiding the toy knife in his jacket or cloak. The assistant has several rubber knives with nails taped to the tips. He hides them in his pants or jacket. Just as the knife thrower fakes a throw, the assistant quickly sticks a toy knife into the flat, bursting a balloon with the nail. It looks as though the knife thrower has thrown the knife and is bursting the balloons—just as it looks as though the whipcracker is splitting the newspaper. The relationship between the knife thrower and the assistant can be exactly the same as in the Whipcracker.

You can apply the elements of the boxing routine—the slapping, falling and the character relationships—to many other situations. Perhaps two bums fight over a barbecued chicken, or a girl clown tries to keep her 2 jealous boyfriends from beating each other up (a la Popeye, Bluto and Olive Oyl).

Guidelines for Creating Your Own Routines

When you're creating your own routines or plots for clown acts, it helps to know the elements of structure and content, and to have a process or procedure for creating them and rehearsing them.

Structure

Structure refers to the way the activities and plot are organized into a routine. All routines should have a beginning, a meeting, an exchange or conflict, a resolution of the conflict, and a departure or exit.

The Beginning—A stylized opening of the routine. Usually it is the entrances of the clowns, as in the Whipcracker.

The Meeting—One clown or more meets another clown, group of clowns, or objects. Very often, the meeting involves a discovery (see page 123). The whipcracker *meets* the assistant when he discovers that she is hiding behind him.

Exchange or Conflict—The characters act upon each other and usually there is a basic conflict in their actions. The whipcracker wants to show off his skill to the audience, but the assistant does the routine wrong out of stupidity and fear. In a solo routine, the conflict can be between the clown and the props, as in the routine of the wire walker, when the chairs keep falling down.

Resolution of the Conflict—The conflict is resolved, or brought to a point where it can no longer be dealt with on stage. When the conflict is resolved, it is usually done in a unique, ingenious, surprising, and funny way. The wire walker resolves it when he moves the chairs close together, for example, so that the rope is on the floor. It becomes impossible to continue the routine in the Whipcracker, when the assistant keeps tearing the paper, which completely exposes the gimmick.

Departure or Exit—This is usually a chase. It should be stylized, punctuating the routine.

Content

The content is made up of many elements of comedy and Clown. All clown routines should have mimicry or imitation, discovery, trickery, stupidity, a slap or a blow, a fall, and a surprise or blow-off. When you explore, improvise or rehearse your own routines, check to see that you've incorporated these elements:

Mimicry or Imitation—The clown might mimic another clown, an animal, another circus performer, audience members, or a character in society.

Discovery—Clowns discover other clowns, objects, and solutions to problems. Moments of discovery are important in clown routines; take your time when you play them. Often clowns discover the obvious.

Trickery—One clown might trick another clown, or clowns might try to trick the audience with a gimmick.

Stupidity—Clowns make stupid mistakes, don't see what is obvious and often get themselves into trouble. Clowns bump into things, trip on things, forget things, and cause all kinds of accidents.

A Slap or Blow—All of the routines in this book contain a slap or blow. Actually, the blow may be more to the clown's ego than a physical slap, as it is in the Whipcracker, when the assistant throws the torn pieces of newspaper into the whipcracker's face. (See page 77 on slaps and falls.)

A Fall—The ultimate blow to a character's ego, especially for an authority figure, is to lose his footing and land on his rear end. (See page 79.) Falls may follow a series of blows or slaps.

A Surprise or Blow-Off—Surprise is one of the most important tools you can use when you want to make people laugh. There can be several surprises in a routine, but the major one should be related to the blow-off (see page 101).

The Process

There is no set formula for creating clown routines and comedy. Eventually, you'll find your own particular method for creating routines. For now, though, use the following outline as a guide:

Notebook—Keep a notebook of ideas and observations (see page 13).

Explorations or Improvisations—When you have an idea that you want to work on, do improvisations and see what comic situations develop out of them. Many funny things happen accidentally and spontaneously in improvisations. Also experiment with different music on tape or on records to perform your routine to.

Write an Outline for the Routine—After you've improvised thoroughly, make some decisions about the activities you want in the routine. Choose your characters and their motivations. Use this outline as a "working script" for rehearsal.

Rehearse—Rehearse what you've written as much as possible. Make changes in the outline as you go along and as you discover new things or activities. Finalize your decision about music and start staging your routine so that it is timed with the music.

Polish—After you've made your decisions about the skit's actions and activities, "clean up" the routine, or polish it. This means you need to go through it slowly and carefully to decide how to stage it so that all your actions and activities are clear. Add props and costumes at this point. Work on your timing. Make sure that everyone in the routine is working together. You may want to count to yourselves, so that you know when to move in relation to your partner. Pin down all of your specific cues. For example, decide when and where to move in a chase scene. Figure out exactly when you want to slow down or speed up the action.

Test It Out—Present your routine to a few friends and see what they think and say. Sometimes friends can be overcritical, so if you make them laugh, you know you're on the right track. If they have suggestions that make sense, you might want to try them out.

Perform—Try the routine in front of an audience.

Rework—Discuss the routine with your partners after each performance. If something went wrong, or if people don't laugh in the right places, try to figure out why. No matter how well the show goes, or how often you perform, there's always room for improvement.

Some Ideas for New Routines

1. Repeat the improvisation with an object, which is described on page 61. Using this chapter as a guide, create a routine with the object.

2. Create a routine about a clown trying to get his hat on his head.

3. Spend an afternoon looking around your neighborhood for humorous incidents and people who strike you as funny. Keep a list of what you see and finally select one to create a clown routine.

4. Create a clown routine based on a fairy tale or legend. For example, you can do a routine about William Tell shooting the apple off his son's head.

5. Create a clown routine about an astronaut and his assistant.

16
creating your image

creating your image

Your makeup and costume comprise the image of your clown. Think of your image as a picture or painting which visually represents your clown's personality and character. Your image is like your trademark. Many clowns are known by their unique image. When you think of Charlie Chaplin, you immediately visualize the little tramp clown which he made famous. Chaplin's tramp is a model of the way in which a clown may express his character through his image. Much of Chaplin's comedy comes from a basic contradiction: the tramp has the mannerisms and affectations of a sophisticated gentleman, but he is, in fact, a starving bum. His costume reflects this. At first glance, it resembles a gentleman's attire, but actually, his tuxedo top is too small; his pants are too big; his cane is broken; his shoes are oversize; and he needs a bath. Yet the little tramp treats his clothing as if it were a brand-new expensive suit. You, as a clown, should also have a special relationship to your costume.

Study pictures of different clowns and note the total effect of their costume and makeup. You can get ideas from pictures of other clowns, but don't copy another clown's image. Your costume and makeup should be an original creation that expresses your own clown and no other.

Your Costume

Start by trying on clothing you find around the house, like your father's old pants or your roommate's funny striped shirt. Then look farther afield. You can find some interesting items in thrift shops. Look in store windows and second-hand stores for pieces of clothing that might go well with your clown.

Charlie Chaplin? No—Charlie Rivels, who won a Chaplin look-alike contest. Chaplin's image became so popular that many professional clowns imitated it.

Harpo Marx' long trench coat helps to project the zaniness of his character. Harpo hides and stores horns, rubber chickens, and a variety of outrageous props inside his trench coat.

Put together a makeshift costume and study yourself in the mirror. Move around with it on and see if it makes you feel funny and, at the same time, connects you to your clown character. Next, rehearse with this makeshift costume and see how it feels. You may discover yourself moving in new ways when you're wearing it, or the costume may inhibit or cover up other movements you've been working on. For example, you'll find it difficult to walk on your hands while wearing an oversize jacket or overcoat. On the other hand, this difficulty might add humor to your routine. Experiment in this way until you develop a suitable costume.

Another approach is to draw a picture of exactly what you want your clown to look like. You can get a professional costumer to make a costume for you from your drawings and ideas. This can be very expensive, and if you change your mind about certain parts of your costume, you'll have wasted money. Only go to a professional costumer if you're sure of what you want and can afford it.

You can also approach student costumers in college theatre departments. They are usually more accessible than established professionals and will do the job for a lot less money. Or you could try asking a relative or friend who knows how to sew to help you out. You may be surprised: your sweet old aunt might get a big charge out of sewing a costume for you.

Another possibility is to buy or find most of your costume, decorate it with frills, and modify and add to it. For example, you can turn an ordinary sport jacket into a clown jacket by sewing on big colorful buttons and adding colorful borders to the sleeves and collar. If you have a striped shirt that you want to use, you can spiff it up by asking a costumer to sew on a collar.

Costume Touches

Here are a few more hints on adding frills and decorative touches to your costume:

Hats—Women's felt hats are great for clown costumes. They come in many different colors and they are considerably cheaper than men's hats. You can bend them in any way you want, attach a flower, or stick in a big safety pin to hold them in different shapes.

Collars—Collars add to the comic effect of your costume. You can have them sewn on too big, too small, or lopsided. You can buy old-time collars in many magic stores. Usually, they're made out of cardboard, but you can use them as patterns for cloth collars.

Ties—Shop around for all kinds of ties. They come in some fantastic prints and sizes. A tie which is too big, too small, or misshapen can add a funny touch to your costume.

Suspenders—Clowns often wear suspenders. Color-coordinate them with your costume. The type that button into place are usually sturdier than the snap or clip-on kind.

Gloves—You can buy colorful work gloves in hardware or department stores. They run in big sizes, and you can create the illusion of comical big hands with them. If you want to wear fancy or dress gloves, try "parade gloves." You can buy them in army surplus stores. They are usually white, but you can dye them any color you like.

Spats—Spats add a nice touch to shoes or sneakers. For example, you can create a comical effect by wearing an old pair of men's shoes, spats, and pants which are too short.

Clown Shoes—Professionally made clown shoes are hard to find. If you can locate professional theatrical costumers, ask them if they know of anyone who makes clown shoes. Also try your neighborhood shoemaker. Or you can make your own shoes. Here are two ways:

The Two-Sneaker Method

Buy a pair of white sneakers that fit you well. Then shop around for an extra large pair of white sneakers into which your smaller pair will fit. Insert your smaller sneakers into the large pair. Glue them in, if you want, to make sure they stay in place. Then wear them as is, or spray paint them a new color.

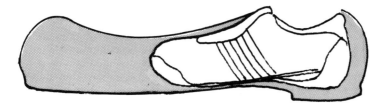

Stuff the empty space in front with newspaper or foam rubber, so that the smaller sneaker fits into the larger one snugly.

The Foam Rubber Method

Carve out an extension to your smaller sneaker from a block of foam rubber. Glue it on the end of your sneaker and spray paint the whole construction.

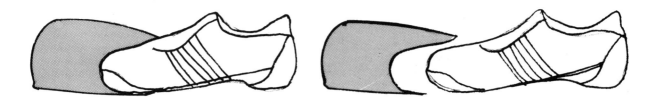

In general, costumes which are too big or small can be funny. One item in your costume might be too big—such as your hat or shoes—while others might be too small, like your tie and pants.

The patterns and colors of your costume are important, too. Whenever possible, use big patterns instead of small detailed ones. Bigger stripes and squares look better from far away or from the stage. Small patterns tend to lose detail on stage, and the colors blend together, creating a mishmash. Don't get carried away, though, with wild and crazy patterns. Always check out the way a pattern looks from a distance before you use it. The same thing goes for your costume as a whole. It might look good close up, but lose all its charm and humor from far away.

Next, you'll find out how to make up your face. In makeup and costume, simplicity is a good rule.

Makeup

Your makeup is the final touch in creating your character. It clearly identifies you as a clown, and audiences will therefore give you the theatrical license to be silly or absurd. It always helps to have neat and professional-looking makeup. On the other hand, no matter how good your makeup is, it won't help if you haven't created a substantial character. Your makeup should enhance your facial expressions and help you project your feelings from far away. Don't hide behind your makeup, and don't create too complicated a makeup. Your makeup should bring out your clown character—not cover it up.

You can buy the items you need for your makeup kit in stores that carry theatrical makeup. They are usually listed in the classified pages of the telephone directory. Sometimes magic stores carry makeup supplies, too.

On pages 146 and 147 you'll find sequence pictures of the application of two different makeups. But first:

A Few Tips

1. If you have very dry skin, apply a very thin film of baby oil to your face before you begin.

2. Hold your hair back with a shower cap, head band or baseball cap turned backwards.

3. Always apply the colors in this order: white, flesh, red, and last, black.

4. Powder after applying each color, and wipe the powder away with your powder brush—except when you want to blend flesh and red.

5. As with your costume, use large simple shapes.

6. Never copy another clown's makeup exactly.

7. Keep your brush clean by dipping it in baby oil after each use. Wipe it clean with a tissue.

8. Clean your hands with baby oil after using each color, and wipe them dry before using another color.

9. Practice making different shapes on your face with the makeup brush. It takes a little practice to learn to draw shapes on your own face and have them come out as planned.

10. Experiment with many different makeups before you select one.

Needed for your makeup kit:

a small tool box (to hold supplies)

a can or tin of clown white grease paint

black grease paint or eyebrow pencil

red grease paint

flesh grease paint

3 makeup brushes

baby powder

powder sock

powder brush (small paintbrush)

baby oil (to remove makeup)

2 clown noses (1 and a spare)

spirit gum (to keep nose in place)

mirror

tissues

cotton swab sticks, such as Q-Tips

baseball cap or shower cap, to keep hair back

11. Before you begin, draw a plan for your makeup on a piece of paper.

12. After you apply a makeup, make faces into the mirror and observe the way your design changes with your facial expressions.

Simple plan for face of the little girl pictured below.

The Whiteface

1. Apply the white makeup to your face with your fingers. Spread it around so that it's smooth. Next, pat the whiteface to smooth it out some more.

2. Wipe away shapes where you plan to apply red and black, using some cotton or a tissue. Then powder, and wipe the excess powder away with your powder brush.

(Powder sets the makeup and keeps it from running or smearing.)

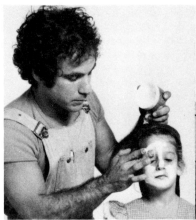

Some clowns cover their necks and ears so that no flesh can be seen.

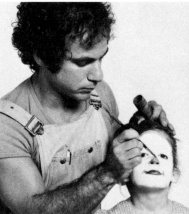

3. Apply red with a brush and then powder with your powder sock.

4. Apply black with a brush or black eyebrow pencil.

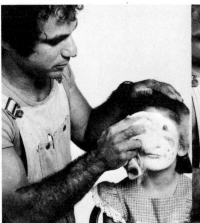

5. Powder your whole face.

Wipe away the excess,

and you're finished.

The Auguste

Apply white carefully with your finger or brush. Tap it lightly and then powder. Use your fingers to apply flesh color. You may want to cover

your neck and ears. Add red shapes and blend in the red with the flesh in certain areas. Powder.

Add black with a brush and powder the whole face. Note: If you're using a clown nose, don't put makeup on your nose.

Last, attach your nose by applying spirit gum to your nose and to the clown nose.

Let it dry a minute and then hold it until it sets in place.

You can also attach a nose with fish line and elastic. Tie the fish line to the clown nose at both ends. The fish line should reach just behind your ears on both sides. Connect the 2 fish lines with elastic. This will provide some give and hold the clown nose in place.

Wigs

You can buy a professional clown wig, custom-fitted and in your choice of colors and shapes. These wigs can be expensive. You can buy inexpensive wigs in all kinds of bright colors in a thrift

148

shop or a department or variety store. You can also dye or spray paint a wig any color you like. Keep your wig securely in place by attaching an elastic strap to the sides.

Trial and error is the key to finding the image that suits you and your character best. You may want to have several costumes for different skits. For example, if your pants fall down in one skit, you'll need a special pair of baggy pants for it. They can be the same pattern and shape as your normal pants, but bigger. In some skits, you might wear a jacket or coat, while in others, you can take it off. Always keep your costume clean and neat, even if it's the costume of a bum or slob. Dirty or smelly costumes can be offensive to an audience.

Exploring and Experimenting with Your Image

It's a good idea to perform a skit with full makeup and costume and ask a friend to take pictures of you. Do the same thing without makeup and costume. Compare the pictures to see the difference.

You may want to perform the same skit twice—with 2 different images. See which one feels better.

Photos on opposite page: (top left) Mike and Beth Bongar, known as Rosie and Herbert, use a whiteface and auguste makeup. Rosie's whiteface has many shapes neatly added with a brush. Triangles, diamonds, squares and circles are often used on the whiteface. The black triangles around her eyes enhance and emphasize her eyes. The soft-red, rouge-like circles on her cheeks suggest an extension of her smile and add a gentle, feminine quality. Herbert's features are exaggerated in the style of the modern auguste. The large white shapes make his mouth and eyes seem bigger. They are outlined in black to accentuate and define their form. (bottom left) Mark Stolzenberg—Your makeup should enhance your facial expressions and personality. Don't use your makeup as a mask which hides your face. (right) Vince Monzo, a modern whiteface clown, moves and behaves like a zany cartoon character. White makeup covers his neck, and he wears white gloves so that none of his flesh is visible. This contributes to his surreal, doll-like look.

clown in perspective

This book has stressed European and American vaudeville, variety arts, and circus styles of Clown. The performers use Mime, magic, stand-up comedy, slapstick, dance, music, circus arts and drama. The clown integrates these arts into a new and unique form through a specific character or performing personality. Clowns create and develop their own material by using traditional theatre forms—scenes and skits—and by trying out new material in front of live audiences. Clowns often use topical issues in their material, and there is a spontaneity and freshness which is part of the clown's improvisational style.

A professional clown is a total actor who is capable of creating, staging, and performing original material. The clown works physically to express him- or herself and stresses surreal, absurd, cartoon-like visual images. This style of performing is simple and direct, and it can be more profound than intellectual or verbal comedy. A good clown shares warmth, love, and insights into the human condition with an audience. Clowns often criticize, mock, and satirize established institutions and authority figures in ways which are socially acceptable. Many cultures have romanticized the role of the clown. Some have granted the clown high status, even a priestly function or position.

For example, Hopi Indian clowns of North America are an elite group of highly skilled tribesmen who mock the rituals of their tribe. The Hopi clowns ride their horses backwards, shoot their bows and arrows the wrong way, and often fall off their horses. They do this to satirize the serious and proud attitude of the tribe towards hunting skills. These same clowns also make fun of individuals in the tribe who have broken the law. They do this during tribal rituals, and the transgressors are so thoroughly embarrassed by their mockery that the ridicule itself is a form of punishment.

In the East there is a strong tradition of clowns performing at theatrical and ritual events. Chinese, Balinese and Indian clowns are given special license to improvise in very traditional, religious, theatrical presentations. These clowns are allowed to speak in the jargon of the common people, break many of the formalities of performing, and usually they are the audience's favorite part of the event.

In medieval times the court jester was often a powerful person. The fool or jester would entertain at court and frequently make fun of the king and other members of the nobility. The jester had the special opportunity to make private matters public by singing songs about the nobility or by telling jokes which related to affairs of state. Some court jesters used their tremendous freedom of expression as a powerful political tool. On the other hand, many court jesters were executed or banished for going a bit too far.

Dan Rice was a popular circus clown in the United States in the 19th century. He was one of Abraham Lincoln's best friends and advised him on many important political decisions. Dan Rice was a skilled animal trainer, strong man, pantomimist, singer, songwriter, equestrian, acrobat, comic poet, folk humorist, and circus owner and manager. He had a tremendous impact on American entertainment and culture at that time, and his clown image was used as a basis for the cartoon image of Uncle Sam.

In the 20th century many great entertainers were schooled as clowns on the vaudeville circuit: artists such as Charles Chaplin; Buster Keaton; Laurel and Hardy; The Marx Brothers; and W. C. Fields. These performers were the leaders in the development of contemporary entertainment, and they had a tremendous influence on the birth of the film industry as an art form.

Almost every culture has had some form of clown entertainment. Perhaps human beings have an innate need to laugh at themselves and at others. Good clowns instinctively play with tensions and conflicts that are a part of human interaction. This provides a healthy, enlightening, and entertaining experience.

Many people believe the cliché that clowns are sad or disillusioned individuals who must make people laugh to overcome their own unhappiness. Or that clowns are running away from harsh realities in their lives, hiding behind their makeup and escaping into the world of fantasy. This is not true. As in every other profession, there are all kinds of people who are clowns. Some are fulfilled in their work and well-adjusted. Others are frustrated and unhappy. However, good professional clowns are highly disciplined artists who spend a lifetime at their craft, and to this craft they add their intuitive or learned insights about human nature.

warmups

Before you rehearse, you need to warm up your body. As a clown, you'll sometimes need to use your muscles vigorously and strenuously. At other times you may need to be graceful and gentle. Sometimes you'll have to tense your muscles; at other times you'll need to relax them. A good warmup routine helps you do all this, and it keeps you from getting sore or pulling a muscle. Do the following warmups before each practice session or rehearsal:

1. Sit quietly and relax for a few minutes before beginning to work.

2. Tuck in your knees and roll easily from right to left. Do it 5 times to each side.

3. Do a shoulder stand, as shown. Stay in this position for one minute.

4. From the shoulder stand, let your legs drop toward the floor near your head. Keep your legs straight and only go back as far as you comfortably can. Don't strain. Then slowly unwind until you're lying flat on your back. Do this twice.

5. Sit on your ankles, keeping your back straight and stretch up. Do this 3 times.

6. Sit, as shown, with your left leg bent and your right leg straight. Stretch up and reach over your right leg. Your chest should sink towards your right knee. Repeat this 3 times slowly. Then do the same thing with your left leg straight and your right leg bent.

7. The Cobra—Lie flat on your stomach with your hands in push up position and your neck touching the floor. Slowly, leading with your head and neck, raise your back as shown. Try to feel each vertebrae in your back move up—one at a time. Keep your pelvis on the floor and use your arms for support and balance. *This is not a push up.*

Slowly come down to the floor, starting with your spine and stomach, and then lowering your chest. Finally, return your neck and head to the floor. Repeat 3 times.

8. Lie on your back and relax. Bring your attention and thoughts to any sensations or stiffness in your body. Do this quietly for 2 minutes.

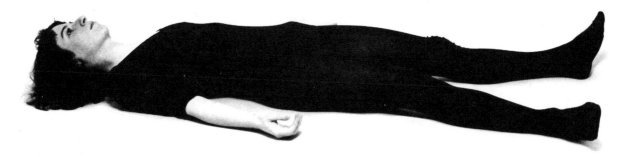

9. Roll onto your hands and knees. Contract and release your stomach and chest, as shown. When you contract (above), round your back like the back of a cat. Do this by pulling your chest and stomach muscles up and in. When you release (below), push your stomach towards the floor. Your back will then be curved in the opposite direction.

10. Get onto your feet and hang from your waist. Keep your arms and neck loose. Slowly, on an 8-count, rise, starting from your lower back, until you're standing straight. Straighten your head and neck last.

11. Do some vigorous activity—such as running in place or jumping rope—until you're almost sweating.

When you do the warmup stretches, don't strain or try to do the exercises perfectly. Do them as best you can in an easy, comfortable way.

Now you should be feeling good and ready for action!

glossary

action expressed as a verb, it describes how a character will go about getting what he or she wants. The character will "convince," for example, "intimidate," or "charm."

activity a sub-action or something specific a character does to carry out an action.

attitude a frozen pose or statue of a clown in the midst of doing something, as if caught in a snapshot.

auguste clown a clown who is foolish, stupid, simple, naive and charming. The auguste's mannerisms and actions are exaggerated, absurd and unpredictable. He or she wears a grotesque, colorful, baggy pants-ed costume, and usually a clown nose.

beat a section of a routine in which a series of activities can be grouped together under one action.

blow-off a surprise and funny ending to a clown routine, usually followed by the exit.

character clown a type of clown which is a caricature of a person or type of person seen in daily life, such as a policeman, tramp, nurse, schoolteacher, and so forth.

circus ring a circular structure which encloses the performing area of a circus.

Clown (also known as "clowning") The art of creating and portraying a specific comical character who uses movement, cartoon-like visual imagery, a specific makeup and costume, satire—sometimes sounds, words and music—and a variety of special skills to entertain and make people laugh.

clown an actor who performs in the style of Clown.

clown character the specific individual a clown portrays.

clown image the visual effect of a clown's makeup and costume.

clown walk the stylized and absurd walk of a clown. Clowns often are identified by their walks.

flat the basic unit of framed scenery.

gimmick a theatrical illusion which clowns create with a special prop. Slap boxing gloves, for example, and Levitation Legs, are gimmicks.

improvise to act out a routine or part of a routine spontaneously. Also to create a skit extemporaneously around a theme or simple idea.

motivating force one basic need which drives a character into action. It is a character's main reason for living, stated as a specific desire for something.

objective what a character wants to accomplish in a specific clown routine. A character's objective helps satisfy his or her motivating force.

powder sock a white sock filled with baby powder which is used to powder the face and set the clown makeup.

project using muscular energy, along with acting technique, to clearly convey your meaning over a distance to an audience.

proscenium stage a traditional raised-platform stage with wings and an arch framing the front of the stage.

slapstick an exaggerated, satirical form of comedy in which clowns use the illusion of physical violence and destruction in dealing with other clowns, objects, situations or themselves.

slow burn a *take* in which the clown expresses that he or she is about to burst open or "burn up" with rage.

slow motion moving at a slower than normal rate, but at a perfectly consistent speed.

spirit gum a liquid which is used to glue clown noses, wigs and facial hair in place.

staccato a sharp, light, quick movement, followed by a freeze.

stylize to exaggerate—to make bigger than life. When you stylize a movement, you use your entire body.

take a reaction with a frozen attitude or facial expression, often done to the audience, in response to something surprising or unusual.

timing the speed and rhythm of actions and reactions.

torms flats or curtains which mask the off-stage areas of a stage.

whiteface clown a sophisticated, graceful, shrewd and aristocratic clown. Traditionally, the whiteface clown wears an elegant costume and white-faced makeup.

wings the area immediately off-stage, left and right.

index

About the Author

Featured on the cover of *New York Magazine* for his highly acclaimed performance in the mime-clown drama "Silent Fantasies," which he co-authored with mime Vivian Belmont (also pictured in this book), Mark Stolzenberg has been electrifying audiences in just about every theatrical medium. After studying acting at the Herbert Berghof Studios and Mime with several different teachers over a period of five years, he attended Ringling Bros. Clown College, and subsequently was chosen to clown with Ringling Bros. Barnum & Bailey Circus. He went on to perform with Bertilino Brothers European Circus and Amandis International Circus. He has made numerous television appearances, acted in films (he co-wrote and played a lead role in "Clowns," a 1920's style silent film), and on stage in many roles (including the one-man, one-act play "Toccata" at the Jean Cocteau Theatre in New York). He has performed in nightclubs and cabarets, at elementary schools, high schools, colleges and universities throughout the Northeast, and if you're lucky you might be able to catch his curbside performance near the entrance to Central Park on a sunny summer day. He teaches classes in mime, clowning and circus skills at his own studio when in New York.